Adoration

John D. Caputo, *series editor*

PERSPECTIVES IN
CONTINENTAL
PHILOSOPHY

JEAN-LUC NANCY

Adoration

The Deconstruction of Christianity II

TRANSLATED BY JOHN MCKEANE

FORDHAM UNIVERSITY PRESS
New York ■ 2013

This book was first published in French as Jean-Luc Nancy, *L'Adoration: Déconstruction du christianisme* 2 @ Éeditions Galilee, 2010.

This work has been published with the assistance of the National Center for the Book—French Ministry of Culture.

Ouvrage publié avec le soutien du Centre national du livre—ministère français chargé de la culture.

Fordham University Press has no responsibility for the persistence or accuracy of URLs for external or third-party Internet websites referred to in this publication and does not guarantee that any content on such websites is, or will remain, accurate or appropriate.

Fordham University Press also publishes its books in a variety of electronic formats. Some content that appears in print may not be available in electronic books.

Library of Congress Cataloging-in-Publication Data is available from the publisher.
Printed in the United States of America
15 14 13   5 4 3 2 1
First edition

Contents

Translator's Note

Let me address a few points of difficulty that recurred throughout the translation.

L'homme can mean both the neutral "mankind" and "man," and although the latter bears a strong whiff of gender determination, it has been chosen throughout in order to convey Nancy's engagement with a historical discourse on the rights of the individual that predominantly referred to men. References to *les hommes* become "men." As for *Dieu*, it presents difficulties not so much in itself but when it is replaced by the pronoun *il*: writing "he" rather than "it" makes more explicit than in the French the personal, anthropomorphized understanding of God. Nonetheless, English forces us to choose: my use of "he" takes into account the tradition of Christian translations and Nancy's engagement with this corpus (in other words, to translate *il* as "it" might be for translation to short-circuit and delegitimize full discursive/philosophical treatment). A third difficulty regards the translation of *être* and *étant*, English proving unusually unresourceful in providing only "being" as a translation for these ontological terms. Glosses are often given in these cases, but where they are not, singular "being" refers to *être* and plural "beings" refers to *étants* (even when Nancy uses what I take to be a collective noun, *l'étant*).

Parole presents its own difficulty, given that it can be translated as "word," retaining a scriptural reference (a common translation of the opening of John's Gospel being "au commencement était la parole"), or as "speech." In part because of its more fluid and mobile connotations, the latter has usually been chosen. Such speech or address can often be found in the form of *salut*. Both functioning as a salutation and meaning "salvation," this word has no equivalent in English, and so throughout the work its presence has been clearly signaled. It is not just language in limited or literal terms that is conceived on the model of salutation and address in Nancy's work, but also sense in general. In this light, sense understood as repetition, transferral, or deferral is present in the French as *envoi* and *renvoi*. The English translations available—"echoing," "referring," "sending," and "dispatching"—cannot reestablish the proximity, itself an echoing, of course, between the two terms. In order to reproduce some of the movement conveyed by *renvoi* in particular, "referring" has often been chosen in place of "reference."

A further close-knit family of terms has had to be separated during its voyage into the English language. The French throbs with terms such as *pulsation, pulsion, impulsion*, not to mention *pousée* and *compulsion* (although the latter, seen as too obsessive, is set aside from Nancy's thinking of the drive to sense). Glosses of these terms have been given where possible, but common translations are "beating" for *pulsation*, "drive" for *pulsion* (thus aligning with Freudian vocabulary in both languages), and "thrust" for *pousée*.

Of course, a work as richly complex as *Adoration* contains many further problems for the translator, even beyond points such as *valeur* (both "value" and "valor"), *partage* (both "sharing" and "division"), *déposition* (at once deposing an authority figure, the act of writing something down or depositing a thesis in a library, and the removal of Christ from the cross). Together with Helen Tartar, whose guidance has been highly stimulating, I have attempted to negotiate these difficulties even as Nancy's text drives itself on to territories new.

Adoration

Prologue

The form of spirit as it awakes is adoration.[1]

Spirit as it awakes is doubtless nothing other than whoever is awaking: whoever has barely emerged from sleep or appeared out of non-existence. It is a spirit perhaps still offended by shadows, deep folds, all that it must set aside and reject in order to become what it is: less breath than penetration, the penetration of a very fine point, whose acuteness, without undoing the impenetrability of matter—the world, bodies, our common presence—nonetheless gives matter its play, its light, not in the sense of what elucidates but in that of what opens up, in that of an orifice opened up amidst compact, common folds.

   At the same time, spirit as it awakes is simply spirit itself. It is nothing other than awakening taken up anew. Freud states that birth lasts a lifetime. Similarly, wakefulness is always reawakening: it does not resolve [*il ne se dépasse*] into a vigilance that is stable, equal to itself. Or rather, as with birth, its resolution [*son dépassement et son aboutissement*] would be, indeed, a simple equality to self that can no longer make a difference either in anyone or between anyone. This equality is death, but spirit—does one dare to say: spirit, or life?—is an inequality to itself of the awakening that opens onto the incommensurable. Here, now, rising to the surface of the equal, the identical, the inherent, we see the unequal, the different, the extrinsic. We see it in such a way that we shall be unable to account for it. That is neither what is proposed nor what is at stake.

1

Being unable to give an account, lacking yardsticks or measures, sensing that there is something beyond the calculable, which cannot be reduced to any commensuration, comprehension, or convention whatsoever. Even not recognizing "what" or "who" is at issue, not recognizing at all but sensing that it is so: that the homogeneous is opened by a heterogeneity beyond any equivalence [*homologie*]—as when, in the moment of awaking, it is possible, briefly, not to know that one is awaking, or where, or when, or why: we all know what that is, even as we also know perfectly well that it *is* not. It is an emotion, a nuance, a word, an allure, a resonance; it is a visage, a birth and a death or sooner, much sooner, it is "one" who is born or "one" who dies. It is the newborn and the dead man insofar as we know that they remain and will remain incommensurable, heterogeneous, irreducible, and, as such, neither "born" nor ever "dead."

This awaking is intermittent, we do not dwell there, or at least we are unaware that we dwell there in another kind of duration and according to another cadence of existence than those that at first account for our being. But this intermittence does indeed rhythm our existence; without it we could not even speak, we would not be the linguistic beings that we are. For we know, as soon as we speak, that language addresses itself and addresses us to this outside of homogeneous communication and signification. That language in its first and last instance addresses itself and addresses us to this heterogeneity, to this outside. Language is there for this alone, it does only this: it addresses, appeals to, calls out to the unnamable, what is strictly the reverse side of all possible nomination. This reverse side is not the world's hidden face, nor a "thing in itself," neither being [*être*] nor being [*étant*]. It does not exist: all existence opens itself starting from it and toward it. "Him," "that [*ça*]," or "nothing": the *thing itself* that is nothing in particular but that there *should be some things, and a world, or worlds, and us, all of us, all existents.*

It is not a reverse side, in truth: it is the very obverse of the real, it is the real as such turned toward us, open to us, and to whose opening we address ourselves. That is what is named "adoration": a word addressed to what this word knows to be inaccessible [*sans accès*].

୬

We know all of this. We know it, and we forget it. Doubtless it is in its nature to be forgotten: and not to be conserved, archived like a document or recorded like a memory. If there were a memory or a document, then we could no longer speak of the "inaccessible," but neither could there any longer be address, no longer could there be this type of approach, of proximity to or even intimacy with the inaccessible. We can even say: there could be no more access to the inaccessible.

Our forgetting therefore keeps intact what nonetheless we know that we touch, that we can touch, or that we sometimes happen to touch—or rather, what touches us, without us truly knowing it, although we are not unaware of it either. Not being unaware of this remarkable possibility that is the very possibility of language, therefore that of our being—that of our being-in-the-world and, by that token, the very possibility of the world. This world touches and/or is touched by the incommensurable, the non-world, the outside. Without which it would not be a world, but simply a universe: a composition of parts made up of elements and dimensions. But the world has neither parts, nor elements, nor dimensions: the world is the exposition of what exists to the touch [*touche*] of sense, which opens within it the infinity of an "outside."

The infinite in the finite. Finitude as an opening to the infinite: nothing but this is at stake. What we call "finitude"—mortality, natality, fortuitousness—would not exist if in the very act of naming it we did not allow it to transpire that we exist and that the world exists as an opening onto infinity, via infinity. This is to say that the very fact of existence prevents existence from being "finite" in the sense of having no extension beyond itself. On the contrary, this fact attests that existence bears, brings with it its entire extension and its full expansion. Here and now, between birth and death, without in any way denying and repressing this "finitude"—that is exactly what *is* infinite: between birth and death, each time, an absolute takes place.

Liberty, Equality, Fraternity, Justice

The appearance here of what we consider to be a political motto, in a form taken from historical variants, may be surprising. A motto, which is to say, a thought that one declares will regulate one's conduct. And yet this quadruple thought—which is perhaps ultimately a single thought—did not appear in history merely in order to regulate a political (and social) mode of conduct. What does it say beyond or before what we habitually hear it as saying?

It says nothing other than this: the characteristics, properties, or qualities recognized as necessarily belonging to members of the human species (let us leave aside for now questions pertaining to other living beings) are not in the first instance characteristics linked to sociality. What's more, sociality understood as the order proper to association and to the balancing out of interests, competences, and conflicts is itself secondary in relation to a resolutely primary given, which is existence in common. The common neither associates nor dissociates, it neither gathers together nor separates out, it is neither a substance nor a subject. The common is the fact that we are—this term being taken in its full ontological import—in an echoing and referring [*renvoi*] from one to the other (yet again, let us leave aside other existents). The element of this echoing and referring is language. Language addresses us to one another, and addresses us all together to what it essentially causes to appear: the infinity of a sense that no signification can fill, and that, let it be said, envelops together with mankind [*les hommes*] the totality of the world with all its existents. Sense is developed, and developed infinitely, only to the degree that this enveloping by the world which makes sense turns back on itself and opens itself within itself according to the configuration named "sense," which can also be said to be "nonsense," "absurdity," or even "inanity [*insanie*]."

The sense of the world is nothing that is guaranteed, nor can we know in advance that it has been lost: it plays itself out entirely in the common echoing and referring that is somehow proposed to us. It is not a "sense" that has references, axioms, or semiologies outside of the world. It is in play insofar as existents—both ones who speak and others—make circulate within it the possibility of an opening, a breathing, an address that is, strictly speaking, the being-world of the world.

When one speaks of "liberty" and "equality"—and of the other notions that are derived from them—outside of social systems in which these notions can be fixed by supposedly natural or divine principles, which is to say, when one speaks of what we name with the overly broad term "democracy," one is in fact, like it or not, bringing these two properties down to what constitutes the humanity of man [*l'homme*], namely, to language.

Men are free and equal insofar as they are speaking beings (and any broader extension of these properties is grasped through language). Of course, this is not to diminish in any way everything that the great tradition of emancipation, liberation, and disalienation meant by these words—whether that be the equality of the right of individuals to own property, to the pursuit of happiness, or to the security and freedom under law of the same individuals to possess, to enjoy, and to engage in ventures (all this accompanied by the requirement that the actual world be modeled on the legal one). It is nonetheless necessary to perceive and to think the provenance and the destination of these characteristics that are proper to a humanity that we can call "democratic," since the word cannot be avoided.

To believe that modern emancipation liberated and made equal individuals who had been repressed by hierarchical, violent, and unjust orders would be a serious mistake. This is another thing that we know but are constantly forgetting (modernity even consists in extending this forgetting). The individual was created in the movement that emancipated him. At the turning point of European civilization, a different humanity was less "liberated" than forged according to a new design. This design did nothing other than wholly expose man to man. It was a design for man and a desire for the truth of man in a world in which all the certainties—and all the fears—that had been maintained as "gods," "empires," and "sacred things" were breaking down.

We have not yet truly perceived what is at stake in this. In the ancient world, when a slave was emancipated, one knew *who* was coming into the picture as a "free man" (I am passing over the details of this "liberation"). When modern man emancipates himself, he does not know *who* he is causing to come into the picture.

This unawareness, or rather, this nescience or non-knowledge, in truth form the stakes, the chance, and the risk in this adventure. We did not receive from any particular direction a *liberty* or an *equality* that we might then have decided to appropriate, with all of these notions' implications of justice, fraternity, and solidarity. Nothing of the sort was simply given to us, and this is why such notions are constantly debated and disputed—as they have been since the Antiquity that prefaced the modern world.

Once we have tested, worn out, and disfigured various figures of "man," of this supposed being whose true existence—I mean his biometaphysical existence as much as his technorelational one—has not ultimately been as well demonstrated as we believe, it falls to us to exceed all figures, configurations, and disfigurations. We don't need more humanism or more democracy: we need to begin by questioning anew the entire thought of "man," returning it to the workshop.

When that is done, we must begin by saying that liberty and equality can only be valid within the element that at first seems to set mankind apart: the use of language. If this use consists in an address turned toward an outside that is not exterior to the world but opens the world in itself, an outside that, when language addresses it, both frustrates address and withdraws access, then such a use is what we must employ. That people have always done so is certain; it is even certain that this is how they began to speak: their first words were words of adoration. Of address and adoration. The first word, or, if one prefers, the first phrase, is straightaway sent beyond its listener and its message: it opens an intrinsic irreducibility in the transmission between the interlocutors, which reveals from within itself that it comes from further back, that it goes further on, and that, whether willingly or not, it sets in motion a surpassing of designation, signification, and transmission.

If the triple god of monotheism essentially speaks (and if Buddha does the same) rather than exercising a power or, put differently, if the exercise of power passes through the word, that is because in god the word takes the place of the exercise and the efficacy of sacrifice. Sacrifice linked one world to another via the spilling of blood. The word opens in the living—in a living being, but for the whole world—an alterity to which it is a question not of being "linked" but of being open. This alterity is not to be named: it is indicated in excess of all names. It is not to be reached [*joindre*]: it forms the joint and juncture of our word, the infinite possibility of sense.

The history that links Mediterranean Antiquity to us shows precisely this. We have effaced the signs of belonging (to a superior realm), and we have disconnected the way things were ordered (the spheres of the worlds, the cycles of time, wisdoms). We have become entirely beings who speak: our word goes nowhere except its own *elsewhere*. Our destiny is henceforth played out there.

Nothing, nobody replies to our word any longer. It is possible that mankind has always known this and always more or less skirted around any admission of it—this skirting around being the figuration of the gods—but that now mankind has come to the point of declaring that nothing and nobody is responding, and yet that everything and everyone resonates with this address that we are.

This address that we all are, in which we have our equality (nobody being able to lay claim to a greater response), our liberty (nobody being able to claim a monopoly on the word), our fraternity (all of us being before the same absence of the "father"), and our justice (everyone being able to expect of everyone that his address be picked up, but not responded to).

Once more, I am intimately persuaded that we know this. Indeed, I would say that it is, in truth, what forms the background to our knowledge of a "mankind" that has for the first time been thrown openly against its very humanity, complete and lacking any mode of recourse save to itself, here, in its time, in its common lack of inheritance.

Real Life Is Elsewhere: Here

Our time is the time of a dispropriation. In it, man finds that he has lost his fondness for himself [*s'y trouve dépris de lui-même*]. Being no longer entrusted to the gods or to science, he can find no confidence in himself.

He is learning that he needs to entrust himself in another way. That he must place trust elsewhere or in others. Turn toward an elsewhere, whether that of Rimbaud's "real life" or of others. But man has only outdated names for any kind of *elsewhere* that could open onto truth: "gods" or "God," "mystery," "beyond," "Tao," "nirvana," "drunkenness," "ecstasy," and also Rimbaud's "clairvoyance," which he himself (Rimbaud the man . . .) put beyond use.

In truth these names are not the only ones to be outdated. All names have this status. Our time displaces or disassembles entire chains of signification. We have only to think of "man," "history," "nature," "law," "science," "love," "art," and there are many more. We live in a suspension of signification.

Incidentally, this is what will always happen to signification: as both the diversity and the mutability of languages demonstrate. But in our time it is sensed more precisely as a sort of breakdown, doubtless because for a long while we had believed in a stabilization, in a permanence of sense that we thought underpinned the displacement of history and the expansion of Western reason. However, in the moment when this expansion is completed with the saturation of the world, the permanence of sense becomes syncopated, and the entire order is put back into play by what one could call "sense."

Indeed, the very sense of this word, the import of this notion, and even—perhaps—its possibility are called into question. But this is how it has always been with sense: it appears only by being called into question, put in play or in crisis. No one and no human culture is unaware of this, nor have they ever been: it is not a given, it is always about to be lost, or else it submerges us. It is always an excess or a lack—but nowhere is there anything against which we might measure sense in order to say whether there is "too much" or "too little" of it. Thus we can say that it is always *just* what returns to us [*nous revient*]. What comes down to "us," speaking living beings, but at the same time to all beings [*étants*], to the whole world in its being launched into the fortuitous swirling of the cosmos amidst nothing.

Mankind has always known and adored the severe grace, the difficult, exasperating, but shocking joy of this senseless, painful, unjust justness.

Addiction—Adoration

"Addiction" is a Latin term to which the English language has given the sense familiar to us. Roman *addictio* is the confirmation of an affirmation, a declaration, a commitment. The word developed its sense in the direction of "to dedicate oneself," "to devote oneself," "to give oneself over to," and later in the direction of obligation, indebtedness, and submission.

It is impossible not to allow some vague relation to emerge between *ab-dicere* (and/or *ab-dicare*, since the two verbs are close to one another here) and *ad-orare*, even though *dire* is related to the declaration and to its content, while *orer* (as Old French had it) suggests speech as address. However, leaving French aside, this sort of brushing contact between the two words can indicate something to us.

If there is a distinctive characteristic of our society, it would seem to be addiction. Some have said that our society is addicted to addiction: indeed, no other culture has known such an extension of the ensemble of addictive phenomena, which, of course, range from serious and less serious drug addictions, to addictions to food or to its refusal (the phenomena of obesity or anorexia), to video games and to the screen in general, to constant listening to prerecorded music, to the unending renewal of excitement caused by fashion, by information, by images of leisure, beaches, tanning, travel, and even to at least one aspect of the speculative vertigo that leads to financial "bubbles" . . .

Pathological dependency is not always to blame, and not always to the same extent—even though tracing the borderline of "pathology" is a dangerous strategy in this area. At the very least, it is a question of *pathos* or *passion*: of a passivity that offers itself as a ready recipient, as ready to be taken up by or in a behavior that responds either to this readiness to be taken, carried off, transported to any available elsewhere or to the demand to be altered in order to be touched, affected, and in that way opened onto an elsewhere.

An elsewhere means sense [*un ailleurs, cela veut dire du sens*], in one way or another. Sense is a referring [*renvoi*] or sending [*envoi*] toward somewhere else, toward others (within or outside me). This is why sense in its essence is incomplete, incompletable, and infinite.

What is the difference between what we are naming "addiction," on the one hand, and "adoration" on the other? It is perhaps very simple.

Addiction, whatever its object or its nature might be, implies a relationship to a tangible, appropriable presence. "Drugs" are what cause me truly to perceive another regime of presence, an "elsewhere" in which I am able to forget or convert the "here" that I wish to leave. In addiction, there is something that ultimately comes down to hallucination.

Adoration signals a relationship to a presence that it would be out of the question to bring "here," that must be known and affirmed as essentially "elsewhere," with the effect of opening the "here." It is therefore not a presence in the accepted sense of the word. It is not the presence of anything in particular, but that of the opening, the dehiscence, the breach, or the breaking out of the "here" itself.

There Is No Sense of Sense

That Is Worthy of Adoration

1

Could one dare to affirm in all seriousness that adoration is what is necessary in the world today?

One could not, and we shall not do so here, even if we feel a certain necessity to do so. We shall not do so partly because it would be grotesque to call for "adoration" in a world that perhaps lacks everything—justice, history, civility [*cité*], splendor, sense—except the idols, fetishes, gods, and celebrities that are proposed as objects of adoration. But this is not the only reason why we shall not simply affirm the necessity of adoration, however self-evident or sensible it might appear, because it is not the right reason.

It not the right reason on two grounds. First, such a reasoning presupposes that adoration could only be addressed to the shimmering and dubious population that has just been listed, those who occupy the altar or the circus ring for a moment only. In truth, we can only learn how things stand with adoration by beginning with a question.

The second ground concerns what it would mean to affirm a necessity. However distressed or anguished our world might be, however disoriented we might have been since we put an end to our sacred and profane eschatologies, the most urgent measure of vigor and truth must not be found in the proclamation of another necessity, merely of a different type. Nothing is necessary for what does not proceed from necessity—and our world proceeds only from its own fortuitousness, or, avoiding the brutality of that word, from its fortuitous character. It is barely acceptable, therefore, to say that it "proceeds from" at all. It takes place, it is there, it could not not be there or not be, it does not derive or stem from anything.

What is to be thought is nothing but this: how the contingent side of existence opens onto an adoration. Not an adoration of itself, as if the fortuitous, the accidental, the aleatory deserved to be set up as something glorious, in opposition to the old necessities, divinities, reasons, and destinations. But rather an adoration of what is not set up on any altar or throne, does not drape itself with glory, and whose setting up, if it takes place at all, is at most also a prostration, a deposition [*déposition*], an abandonment.

Nothing is more familiar to us than to lament the threat hanging over the world and existence—and this is more than just a characteristic of our tradition, even if it was considerably reinforced when Sophocles, in Hölderlin's understanding of him, said that man is "monstrous . . . [he who] offends the laws of the World and of the faith/that is sworn to the Powers of Nature."[1] Since Sophocles, we have been excavating the monstrous and finding the absurd, and we have been losing laws, such as faith in all the Powers. We often repeat: "Sometimes I believe that nothing has meaning. On a minuscule planet that has been heading toward oblivion for millennia, we are born in pain, grow up, struggle, fall ill, suffer, cause suffering, cry out, and die: we die and at that very moment, others are born in order to start the useless comedy anew."[2]

Even if this is familiar, Sophocles and Sabato wrote it anew. They wrote, and we take literature into consideration not because it is a transcription of data but because it opens and communicates possible, indeterminate, uncompletable meanings.

2

The fortuitous character of existence—that of the world as well as that of each being [*étant*], whether speaking, living, or inert—is not the same as its contingency. The latter is still measured via the contrast it opens up with necessity. *Contingency* is a philosophical term, and as such it is already engaged in a dialectic whereby the totality of what is contingent can form a general order of the world. The "fortuitous" puts forward a notion less of a nature or a state than of a circumstance, a movement. In a fortuitous way, something happens, and something falters in its fortuitousness or in its fortuitude. It is a fortunate encounter (the same word is there, *fors*), which can be good or bad—and the good encounter at all times lays itself open to the off-beat of the bad.

Essentially, what is fortuitous responds to a discontinuous and fleeting conception of time. It responds to the discontinuity as much of singularities themselves as of the modes—space/time—according to which this discontinuity becomes singular.

This is nothing new: what is fortuitous, together with what is fleeting, elusive, ephemeral, and lacking in substance, composes the minor rhapsody of our system of references, whose major mode looks for what is stable, constant, and durable. This enables us all the more to have a presentiment of the moment at which the fortuitous summons us: summons our adherence, which, however, finds nothing to which it can adhere.

It finds nothing to which it can attach itself, to which it can hold, nothing in which to inscribe a profession of faith or a grounded assurance. It finds nothing but fortune, its turns, its obverses and reverses. Not Fortune as a blind goddess who plays with our destinies, but this fortune of our lots [*sorts*], which is to say, that of our existences thrown into the world just as what were called *sortes*, blocks of wood that were suddenly detached from a string, were thrown. Our existences, which we neither bear nor bear up, thrown for no reason across the void that alone unites them, that gathers them via its enigma—or via its very clear obviousness [*évidence*]. Our existences, all of them, those of humans and of other living beings, those of the elements that support them or provide them with an environment, with food or instruments—the air, minerals, water, fire, electrons, magnetic fields. These existences are linked only by their common projection, which creates a world and a world of differentiated worlds—which is to say, an ensemble or a network of possibilities of sense.

Sense is a referring [*renvoi*] (a relation, a ratio, an address, a reception—a sensibility, a sentiment). A world is a totality of echoes, but it does not echo [*renvoie*] anything else. The worlds within the world—for example, the worlds of the polar circles or of classical Indian music, the worlds of Goya or of Wittgenstein, of caterpillars or of transistor radios—form "the" world by echoing and referring among themselves: but "the" world refers to nothing.

There is no other world, no world beyond, nor any "backworld" ["*arrière-monde*"] (Nietzsche). This means that there is no ultimate reference for the network of the world's references, and that therefore there is no (ultimate) Sense of sense or of the senses.

There is no sense of sense: this is not, ultimately, a negative proposition. It is the affirmation of sense itself—of sensibility, sentiment, significance: the affirmation according to which the world's existents, by referring to one another, open onto the inexhaustible play of their references, and not onto any kind of completion that might be called "the meaning [*sens*] of life," "the meaning of history," or even "salvation [*salut*]," "happiness," "eternal life," no more than it opens onto the supposed immortality of works of art, which are in themselves nothing other than forms and modes of reference. Yet our true immortality—or eternity—is given precisely by the world as the place of mutual, infinite referral.

Adoration speaks of this infinite that speaks to it, addresses it. It is, in a way, the praise of infinite sense.

3

A praising that is itself without end, a praising commensurate with what it praises—and equal to what it praises, since it stems from there. Commensurate with an incommensurable.

For this reason it is neither possible nor desirable to discuss adoration in an organized, coherent way. But neither is it a case of privileging what is unorganized, fragmented, suspended. One can only attempt approaches—or follow glimpses—that might lead toward something that we cannot even classify as a "theme."

Undoubtedly, adoration must not be thematized. And in any case, if this project—this meditation—is exploratory, this does not mean that it will explore the possibilities of a "theory" of adoration; rather, it will follow through those of nothing less than a praxis. This praxis bears an unexpected name: thinking. Indeed, thinking should not be conflated with intellectual activity—the establishment of relationships, the invention of nominations (concepts) and of arguments (reasons)—nor with individual activity (judgment, appreciation, evaluation). Thinking is a movement of bodies: it begins in the folded-over nerves [*ce pli nerveux*] of the body and is exposed to the infinite of a *sense*, which is to say, of affection coming from other bodies.

The body arouses thinking through all its sensitive modes of access [*accès*]—sensory, sentimental, sensible [*sensés*]—and thinking forms the supplementary access: the one that opens all the senses onto the infinite. This does not mean that all the senses feed into a unique sense that would subsume them all. The diversity of the sensory apparatus—as well as the difference between the sensory, the sentimental, and the sensible—remains in the infinite and thus keeps the infinite open, inexhaustible, and excessive [*surexcédant*].

Such is the incommensurable to which we are exposed: it is not merely incommensurable with us and with all other beings [*étants*], but also with itself. Such is the chance and the *jouissance* of thinking: that it should be essentially a relationship to excedence itself, to the absolute excedence that can be named "being" [*l'"être"*] but also "world" or "sense." Excedence of all that is given, but also of itself: excedence of the gift upstream from the given. The gift of this: that there are some things, things, all beings [*étants*]—but not "something rather than nothing," since precisely *nothing* is what there is, in place of the gift.

4

> It is because there is nothing else I
> believe there is something else.[3]

The gift of the world calls for adoration. It invites us to adoration, commits us to it, arouses it. But what's more, this gift opens the possibility—if not the necessity—of adoration. Not that it obliges us, as a giver can oblige the receiver. But this gift without giver, this gift that in itself is simply equal to the event of the world, already in itself constitutes a gesture of adoration: this gift turns towards the infinite, or rather, it bears to the infinite the *real* of the *nothing* of which it is the dis-enclosure.

Here it could be shown how this *realization* of *nothing* does nothing but gloss the doctrine of "creation ex nihilo." But it is not necessary to make a detour through this theology, which might always appear to be pulling us obstinately toward a divine omnipotence.[4]

It is sufficient to say: rigorously, a "creator" of course is conflated with his act of creation, and this act is conflated with a fortuitous rupture in nothingness. *Ex* does not mean "beginning with," but rather "outside of," "at a distance from." A distance comes about [*survient*], comes into play within homogeneous, undifferentiated nothingness. Whether it comes about "at a given moment" or "during all eternity" comes down to the same thing, and yet it *comes about*. It is the very fact of coming about. This gap opens the world.

To the objection that a gap is produced "within" something, one could reply that indeed *nihil* and *something*—the undifferentiated thing, the "void" of which metaphysicians speak, the datum that is archepremier, sub-atomic, or however one wants to describe matter[5]—are identical. *Nihil* would thus be spacing itself, the tension of the gap, the beating [*pulsation*] or drive [*pulsion*] that causes it to open up. In this view, then, there is no difference between a full understanding of well-known theologies (perhaps

14 ■ **There Is No Sense of Sense**

mystical ones . . .) of creation and the affirmation of the atemporal permanence of a matter—or an energy—that is always already given, always already *there*. At each instant of time this *there* is there, opened as an *ex*.

This world that opens up is not a "possible world," since no projection
of possibilities has preceded it: nothing, in the heart of nothingness, draws
up the plans or the hypotheses of any kind of world. Instead, the world is
the improbable rupture, the separation of day from night, of waters from
earth, of this molecule from that, of this existence from that. *Ex nihilo* is
each configuration of crystals, each convolution of the nervous system,
each physiological rhythm, each combination of thought, of machines, of
computational systems, or of musical compositions.

What is produced is a gap, a rupture from what could have remained
within an inherent, closed identity—in truth, one should not say "identity" but idiocy: closed on itself, but without any inside nor outside,
bogged down in itself. Rupture opens identity by way of difference and
the inside by way of the outside, day by night, and nothing by things. But
in itself it is nothing, nothing but a gap, an opening. The infinitesimal
reality (*res*, nothing [*rien*]) of opening. And therefore also of relationship,
transport, transformation, or exchange, of the fortunate or unfortunate
encounter. The opening is as risky, as adventurous as it is fortuitous, as
dangerous as it is precious.

Adoration is addressed to this opening. Adoration consists in holding
onto the *nothing*—without reason or origin—of the opening. It is the very
fact of this holding on.

Adoration therefore carries itself with a certain humility. As the tradition knows in various ways, "ex nihilo" also means that God makes something of the most humble, of almost nothing, with no regard for what is
powerful and remarkable. Humility, whether it be Jewish (Job), Christian
("for he hath regarded the low estate of his handmaiden"/"respexit humi-
litatem ancillae suae"; Luke 1:48), or Muslim ("Islam": a trusting submission) has nothing to do with humiliation. It measures an infinite distance,
nothing else.

5

There is something in this thought—the extreme point of all thought—
that belongs to all forms and all epochs of culture, religion, and philosophy. (It is the point at which each touches the other, yet spaces itself at
the moment of doing so, since religion fills in the *nothing*.) But there is
also a characteristic that becomes sharper and more accentuated in the
modern age.

This is shown in a text by Kant—a text that of course still bears the marks of an age preceding modernity but which we can transpose in order to bring it closer to us.

Kant writes:

> Thus the consideration of the profound wisdom of divine creation in the smallest things and of its majesty in the great whole, such as was indeed already available to human beings in the past but in more recent times has widened into the widest admiration—this consideration not only has such a power as to transport the mind into that sinking mood, called *adoration*, in which the human being is as it were nothing in his own eyes, but is also, with respect to the human moral determination, such a soul-elevating power, that in comparison words, even if they were those of King David in prayer . . ., would have to vanish as empty sound, because the feeling arising from such a vision of the hand of God is inexpressible.[6]

This can be transposed as follows:

> Confronting a world in which he can see no finality, man has always been struck by the sentiment of an organized cohesion, both in the smallest details and in the majestic scale of the universe and its history. This admiring astonishment grew with modern science's penetration into all dimensions of the world, though at the same time science withdrew infinitely any kind of sufficient reason. Thus it is that, when confronting his own place and his own role in the unending ecotechnical transformation of the world, man feels this sentiment. This contemplation or consideration harbors a force that plunges us into the sentiment of our own nothingness at the same time as it asks that we be equal to this excedence of ourselves and of all worldly significations.

Adoration is a relationship to excess where ends and reasons are concerned, a relationship to existence as this excess itself—just as much for the existence of the world as for the existence of life, thought, and any kind of tension going beyond intention. Where Kant was able to name the hand of God—in order to declare it inexpressible—we name a tension without intention: the fortuitous as our fortune, the contingency of the gap opened in *nothing* and making a *world* without a purpose, without a destination, but giving us a destiny by that very token—and what a powerful destination, with what a dispatching force [*force d'envoi*]!—the destiny to take up this tension without intention, this potential for an existence without essence.

Perhaps what Derrida named "destinerrance" should be understood in this way: destination is not to go anywhere in particular, but to displace ourselves on the spot in this place of all taking place, where we exist with the totality of existents, to displace ourselves along (or around, in the proximity of) this tension, this ex-tension and this thrust (drive, beating, rhythm) that orders and organizes the very fortuitousness of a "taking place" without reason or end. From the crystal to logic, there is an ordering and an organization for which no design can account but whose very tension—crystalline, organic, living, thinking—tightens toward our attention: not in order to resolve it, but in order to come to meet it, in order to experience it. This is what we call "thinking."

Or "adoring." Which is to say, standing in relation to this *nothing* of reason or ends, of substance or the subject, of caution or accomplishment.

🙠

This emptying out of the principle and the end also intimates that we must not be content with thinking "creation" as an initial event, nor as a single event. Creation is constantly taking place, as could be illustrated by speaking of particles coming into contact with one another or of exploding stars, of living species, or of human inventions. What takes place at every moment is what Descartes called "continuous creation": the putting into play [*jeu*], if one might say so, of the game [*jeu*] itself, this game that throws and throws again the dice of a "taking place" that is always resumed in new metamorphoses. Undoubtedly, we must then ask ourselves how human inventions pursue this game, or whether they reverse its sense, if they endanger the creativity of living beings and the equilibria of their vital milieus. In this sense, the question of ecology is as metaphysical as it is practical. But precisely the fact that this question is being asked and that we cannot avoid worrying about "the greenhouse effect," deforestation, and overfishing means two things: on the one hand, that "nature" itself—because mankind issues from it—can engender a "denaturing" and that no law or "natural" or "providential" design can be invoked to regulate the course of a creation capable of turning against itself; on the other hand, that technology [*la technique*] can rightfully be considered to be the renewal of creation and of its absence of fixed ends. The contradiction between these two envelops the necessity, now starkly revealed, of thinking the absence of any metaphysical necessity—and how this absence commits us.

6

Adoratio: the word as it is addressed. *Oratio*: a solemn word, a word maintained [*tenue*] before anything else, a tension of the voice, of the mouth, and of the entire speaking body. A word whose content is inseparable, if not indiscernible, from the address. An elevated language that is distinguished from *sermo*, ordinary language.[7] A prayer, invocation, address, appeal, plea, imploring, celebration, dedication, salutation. And more precisely, not one or another of these registers, but a composition formed from them all. And lastly, or first of all, a salutation [*salut*]. Yes, the simple "hi!" ["*salut!*"] participates in adoration. When Derrida writes, or rather cries out, with all his might, "*salut!*—a salutation without salvation,"[8] he indicates the following: that the word addressed, the address that barely contains anything beyond itself, bears the recognition and affirmation of the existence of the other. It does nothing more than that, nothing that could be taken up or sublimated into a superior order of sense or of dignity: for this existence is sufficient in itself, it is "safe" ["*sauve*"] in itself, without needing to exit from the world.

This existence makes sense or *is* sense, and with it the whole world can make sense, from "salut!" to "salut!," from one to another. Do not the morning sun, the plant pushing out of the soil, address a "salut!" to us? Or the gaze of an animal? And as for us, how do we salute one another? Is there not salutation in the dispatches, the addresses that we exchange with one another—for example, in the signals formed by buildings, towns, clothes, or objects? And of course in the signals found in the delivery of a piece of information, in establishing communication, whether by telephone, radio, television, or the Internet? There is no reason to think otherwise. We interpret technology as a combination of instruments: but it is just as much an exchange and a propagation of salutations.

If we think, however, that we ought to save technology or save ourselves from it, that is because we are unable to distinguish between its submission to ends and its independence from those ends. Whenever there is a project, a program, or an indefinite accumulation of always-renewed ends that share a common profitability or productivity, there is also an instrument. One cannot salute whatever is produced, insofar as the product enters into general exchange, into the circulation where all "products" are equal on some level, when they act as merchandise and therefore as currency, as something that can be multiplied and invested, but not saluted. That is what "capitalism" is: the substitution of invested, productive riches for glorious, unproductive ones.

Civilization chose this substitution, unconsciously of course, a choice that was not decided by one person, but which has engaged the history of the world for at least six centuries. And to remain with our current topic: this choice implies a sort of turning away from the principle of adoration. It is not by chance that, from the "golden calf" to the outdated miser and up to the present entrancement of traders with the profits made possible by the movement of huge virtual bodies of money, certain elements of a caricatural adoration appear: admiration, veneration, fascination, alienation in all senses of the word—for it is all a question of madness. This madness falls into a pattern that is exactly the reverse of the other madness present in adoration: the madness of relating to a value without equivalent, to a sense outside of sense. Which is to say, to the world and to existence.

The indefinite proliferation of technological ends—speed, digitalization, the command of space, the culturing of stem-cells, genetic modification and all that this appears to threaten—can be related to nothing other than its own indefiniteness or that of the profits that can be made from this proliferation. But what is necessary above all, at the heart of civilization, is the opening provided by what can today no longer be called a "transcendence" without seeming to turn toward a God that is dead and toward "backworlds" ["*arrière-mondes*"].

Nonetheless, "transcendence" is what is at issue, however little the uniquely dynamic nature of this term is understood: it does not designate the status of a "being" ["*être*"] that would be supreme to a greater or lesser degree, but rather the movement whereby an existent leaves behind its simple equality to itself. Which means: to *ex-ist* in the full sense of the word.

But it is true that the word *transcendence* is burdened with centuries of usage in a static, non-dynamic sense, and hence it can be abandoned. Indeed, it must be, because it is by changing words that thinking can be dislocated—and in dislocating thinking, what I have given the burdensome name of "civilization" can also be dislocated. The resulting weighing down of words, the burden of meanings, and the ensuing kind of paralysis of language are themselves signs that a culture is becoming enclosed within a homogeneity that renders it insignificant for itself (or that means it is significant only for itself: technology equals technology, money equals money, law equals law, and being equals being, etc.). "To adore"—I am aware that this word is even more burdened than others, overburdened with dubious piety and with worldly frivolity—must also and perhaps most of all be a way of addressing differently words that we can only rarely change or replace as we might like. A neologism is technically a bright idea, a useful tool, but it only enters into language if it is taken up by usage.[9] And usage depends on the dispositions and deep currents in "culture" or "civilization." Neologism or the reuse of a word—"paleonymy," as Derrida said—always involves an attempt to move within language, to move language, but it is only language that can truly move. Language alone: thought, culture, their imperceptible movements, the dislocations and the metamorphoses of sense and how it appears.

"Adoration" simply means: attention to the movement of sense, to the possibility of an address that would be utterly new, neither philosophical nor religious, neither practical nor political nor loving—but attentive.

Attentive, for example, to the fact—one of thousands that could be cited—that whereas the Qu'ran states that God created mankind in order to be adored, modern man is ready to condemn the nullity of this vain operation, the exorbitant presumptuousness of such a Narcissus.[10] But what if we were called upon to understand the Qu'ran's statement altogether differently? What if it meant that "God" is only the name adopted by a pure excess—indeed vain, indeed exorbitant—of the world and existence over themselves, in themselves? Of a purely and simply infinite relationship to infinity?

꒱

To adore is not to pray in the sense of asking for something or in those of imploring or supplicating, commending, confiding, dedicating, or devoting; neither is it to honor, praise, celebrate, or idealize; neither is it to glorify or to exult; it is not to sing, even though singing is to pray twice (Augustine); it is none of the above, nor what praying might appear to be in any other way. But it is also all of the above, indistinctly, augmented—or rather modulated—by a breath, an aspiration, an inspiration, and an expiration whose three motions come to constitute, most simply, breathing. The model of pneumatic prayer practiced by some Orthodox monks comes to mind. And doubtless we should consider the *pneuma*. We could begin by saying that *pneuma* is what does not speak, without being silent either. Not words, but the breath that carries them. And the trace of this breath in us, in the other. A word of breath [*parole de souffle*].

꒱

Adoration is addressed to what exceeds address. Or rather: it is addressed without seeking to reach, without any intention at all. It can accept to not even be addressed: to be unable to aim, or designate, or recognize the *outside* to which it is dispatched. It can even be unable to identify it as an outside, since it takes place here, nowhere else, but here in the open. Nothing but an open mouth, or perhaps an eye, an ear: nothing but an open body. Bodies are adoration in all their openings.

"Here in the open": this is henceforth the world, our world. Open to nothing other than to itself. Transcendent in its own immanence. Invited, called, no longer to consider its reason for being but rather to confront the dis-enclosure of all reasons—and of all cynical, skeptical, or absurd unreason—in order to measure itself against this: that this world alone, our world, provides the measure of the incommensurable. Its contingency, its fortuitousness, its errancy are only fragile names, linked to the regime of sufficient reason, that attempt to say a reason that is not insufficient (it is not an abyss, though it has no bottom), but rather overflows all sufficiency, exceeding all satisfaction.

This world is indeed ours, everyone's. Here I speak starting out from what is called the Western tradition—Greek, Latin, Jewish, Christian, Muslim—without forgetting that henceforth the "West" no longer exists: finding itself everywhere, it is no longer anywhere in particular. The propagation of its reason throughout the whole world annuls—broadly speaking, but it is precisely a question of broadness—what was its domination. Domination henceforth takes on different forms, and the division of the weak and the strong—which was, of course, given structure by the economic and technical rationality of the West—is articulated in a wholly different and more complex way than any domination of the world by one part of it. Globalization is also a deterritorialization—in this sense, it undoes the "world" in the latter's accomplished, ordered, cosmic, and cosmetic senses—and this deterritorialization gives us cause to think, beyond any representation of the relationships, conflictual or otherwise, between civilizations, about the stakes of a mutation that affects the world as such, in any sense we could give to that expression.

Do other traditions—Buddhism, Taoism, for example—provide different resources with which to face the same stakes? Some want to believe so, but their disposition often appears so voluntaristic as to seem dreamy. If the stakes are the same for everyone and if they are based in a rationality—fortuitously—formed in the regions of the setting sun, one might think that it is difficult not to take into account the genealogy of this "reason." Can we, for example, pass up something recognized as a right by all? In commerce it is impossible, and it will become so in other domains, for other modes of commerce (although this does not mean that "human rights" will always refer to the same "man" as conceived by the same "Enlightenment"). But it will refer to a humanity whose at once fortuitous, ungraspable, and infinite nature we need to think about more. In any case, I can only speak from the position of the old European humanism as it questions itself.

In the Midst of the World

MANDORLA
In the almond—what dwells in the almond?
Nothing.
What dwells in the almond is Nothing.
There it dwells and dwells.

—Paul Celan

Why Christianity?

Why speak of Christianity?

In truth, I'd like to speak of it as little as possible. I'd like to move toward an effacement of this name and of the whole corpus of references that follows it—a corpus that is already mostly effaced or has lost its vitality. But I do think it is important to follow the movement that this name has named: that of an exit from religion and of the expansion of the atheist world.

This world, our world, that of what used to be called "Western" civilization, which can now be distinguished as such only by vestiges of language or by divisions in which the "orient/occident" distinction plays only a small part—it is no accident that this world was first built up as "Christendom" [*chrétienté*]. Christianity was much more than a religion: it was the innervation of a Mediterranean space that was searching for a nervous system after it had put in place the morphological and physiological system of law, the city, and reason. Indeed this ternary—law, city, reason (we can also include art)—was a translation of the disappearance, with which the ternary itself was faced, of any assurance [*assurance*] concerning the foundation of existence. That is to say, any assurance concerning what we can also designate as the presence of the gods. It was the Greeks who perceived the absence of the gods in the place of this presence.[1]

We can say this in a different way, in order to move toward an essential characteristic of Christianity. The Greco-Roman world was the world of mortal mankind. Death was irreparable there; and whether one tried to think about it in terms of glory or in terms of deliverance, it was still the incompatible other of life. Other cultures have always affirmed death as another life, foreign yet close by, strange yet compatible in various ways. Irreparable and incompatible death struck life as an affliction. Christianity, reinterpreting an aspect of Judaism, proposed death as the truth of life and opened up in life itself the difference of death, whereby life could know itself as immortal and "saved."[2]

That life can be saved, or better still, that its salvation should be a certainty has been interpreted in many ways—by martyrdom, by ascesis, by mysticism, by the mastery and possession of nature, by adventure and enterprise, by the search for happiness, by the "emancipation of humankind"—and we will come back to what this "salvation" [*salut*] might still mean to us, what it still has to tell us. The turning point of civilization that reenergized "the West" was played out around what was called "eternal life." However, *eternal life* is not life indefinitely prolonged, but life withdrawn from time in the very course of time. Whereas the life of ancient mankind was a life measured by its time, and the life of other cultures was a life in constant relation to the life of the dead, Christian life lives, in time, what is outside time. This characteristic seems to have an intimate relation to with what I am calling here adoration, which I could characterize as a relation to the outside of time (to the pure instant, to the ceasing of duration, to truth as an interruption of sense).

But before coming back to the motif of salvation [*salut*], we must lay out what is contained in this proposition: "Christianity" is life in the world outside of the world. Nietzsche (to invoke the best witness to this subject) understood it perfectly. This despiser of "backworlds" [*arrière-mondes*] knew that Christianity (at least in a version of it to which no Gospel or Church ever truly conforms) consists in being in the world without being *of* the world. This is to say that it does not limit itself to adhering to inherence, to what is given (whether this is taken as the "real" or, on the contrary, as an "appearance"). Two of Nietzsche's well-known figures illustrate what he sometimes claims to be the "experience at the heart" of Christianity: the tightrope dancer and the child playing with dice. Neither relates to the world as a given by which she is surrounded; on the contrary, they relate to that in the world which makes an opening, rift, abyss, game, or risk.

"Life in the world outside of the world" is so far from being an exclusively "Christian" formula that it finds an echo [*répondant*] in the statement by Wittgenstein that "the sense of the world must lie outside the world."[3] Of course, Wittgenstein is not calling on any representation or conception of "another world": he is asking that the outside be thought and grasped in the midst of the world.

What is thus shown by Nietzsche and Wittgenstein could be shown by a thousand other references. The "spirit of Christianity" (to quote Hegel) is none other than the spirit of the West. The West (which—need it be said?—no longer has any distinct circumscription) is a mode of being in the world in such a way that the sense of the world opens up as a spacing [*écartement*] within the world itself and in relation to it. This mode can be distinguished both from the mode in which sense circulates in the world without discontinuity—death as another life—and from the mode whereby sense is circumscribed in the narrow space of a life that death dispatches to insignificance (a dispatch that can shine with the brief splendor of tragedy). Of course, the Western mode brings with it the great danger of an entire dissipation of sense when the world opens onto nothing but its own chasm. But this is precisely what concerns us.

Where initially there had been an uninterrupted circulation between life and death, then a tragic celebration of mortal life, what was produced and put an end to this—an end to what we call "Antiquity," which is to say, the first epoch of the "West"—was what a historian describes as "the huge divide which all late antique thinkers, pagan, Jewish, and Christian alike, saw between the 'upper' and the 'lower' world."[4]

For the moment, then, this: "Christianity" has developed and modulated the theme of this "immense fracture" and, on that basis, has engendered the intimate constitution of our "mundane," atheist civilization, with its indefinitely dispersed ends [*fins*]. We exited from Christendom long ago, but that only serves to confirm this particular constitution. It is not a question, then, of being somehow interested in Christianity for itself, or for some religious, moral, spiritual, or saving virtue in any of the senses that the professions of Christian faith have left us with. In order to end, we give what remains of Christianity its leave, and this is why we can maintain that it is deconstructing itself.

But in deconstructing itself, it dis-encloses our thinking: whereas Enlightenment reason, and following it the reason of the world of integral progress, judged it necessary to close itself off to all dimensions of the "outside," what is called for now is to break the enclosure in order to understand that it is from reason and through reason that the pressure, the drive (this *Trieb* of reason that Kant wants to uphold)[5] of the relation with the infinite outside comes about, and does so *in this very place*. Deconstructing Christianity means opening reason to its very own reason, and perhaps to its unreason.

ॐ

A few words more about the other branches of Western monotheism, as well as, in a more lateral way, about Buddhism.

What I am saying about Christianity does not confer a privilege upon it, nor does it place Christianity at the top of some list of honors. Rather, it comes down to indicating Christianity as the least privileged of religions, the one that retains the least well, with the most difficulty, the energy that is strictly speaking religious, that is to say, the energy of a sense that is able to carry on from life to death and back again. And it is no accident, if what I have said above is granted, that Christianity has desacralized, demythologized, and secularized itself in such a constant and irreversible way for at least six centuries—if not for far longer. (Should we not say: from the moment Christendom existed, it entered into deconstruction and dis-enclosure?)

"Christianity" is nothing more than a name here—and a highly provisional one—for "us": for what makes us the bearers of this being outside the world in the world. "We" who have borne the entire world to this "civilization" that not only knows "discontentedness" (*Unbehagen; malaise*), as Freud said, but henceforth recognizes itself precisely as discontentedness in the guise of civilization. Discontentedness: because we no longer know what makes us "civilized" or even what this word should indicate. Because we can no longer be sure that our civilization does not engender itself as barbarity.

During a certain period we believed that Christianity was the malady of the West. Not only did we think that reason would cure us of this malady, but we expected from reason the true flowering of what the Christian message had no sooner announced than betrayed: justice in fraternity, equality in the distribution of wealth and in a common destination, the election and dilection of the singular individual and of everyone together. In truth, everything that we called "humanity"—using a word that named both the species of speaking beings and the ideal of rational beings—proceeded from Christianity insofar as it was an assurance that the other life was opened up in life itself and in its death.

What we can understand today is that, if there is malaise or malady, it was not produced by a religion which would have infected the Western body. It is this body itself that is ill, if there is illness, and the task of treatment belongs entirely to it—a body henceforth extended to all humanity, and further, to all heaven and earth—whether we are thinking in terms of healing, conversion, metamorphosis, grafting, or mutation. It is necessary to extract from Christianity what bore us and produced us: it is necessary, if possible, to extract from a ground deeper than the ground of the religious thing [*la chose religieuse*] that of which religion will have been a form and a misrecognition [*méconnaissance*].

ᴣ

This is why I am not setting up any competition between Christianity, Judaism, Islam, and Buddhism. Only Christianity produced itself as the "West," and it alone diluted its confessional features and disintegrated its religious force in this West, for better or for worse. It is out of the question to deny the genius proper to each of the three other religions and their contributions to the thinking and splendor of mankind. What's more, one could say that all three have withheld themselves from the process of "civilization"—by engaging in it either not at all or very little, or, alternatively, by instilling vital energies that, as they became detached from their religious sources, came to give nourishment to civilization (such as Arabic science and philosophy, Jewish meditations on speech and on the flesh, the Buddhist discipline of detachment and compassion).

To become detached from the source and observance of religion was to become detached from all the ways of relating to death as the outside of life, or as its extension: it was to adopt the possibility that the other of life could open up within life itself and unto life itself—to the point of running the risk, as we do from now on, that all that opens up is a chasm into which life plunges. As a religion, Christianity delivered the message of this opening in an equivocal way: it promised a life found anew in the afterworld, and it also proposed frequenting the dead via the communion of saints. The Christian religion mixed together all the characteristics of religion—and the other religions are by no means wrong about its impurity, which they denounced and which was also denounced from within Christianity. In truth, Christianity unceasingly reforged the sacred link and religious observance, because its destiny as a *religion* depended on them (all the more because Christianity had in fact invented the status of "religion" as an instance and institution of salvation, as distinct from civil religion as it was from philosophical atheism). There would be no end to a list of all the dogmatic contents and all the spiritual tonalities that reforge the link between life and death and turn away as much from "death opened in the midst of life"—another way of saying "life in the world outside the world"—as from incompatible (tragic) death.[6] Certain moments or aspects of Christianity enable us to see this, such as the Orthodox tradition or the most initiatory or magical aspects of the Roman Catholic tradition (sacraments, ecclesiastical authority), or even the various puritanisms. Here and there, in various ways, it has always been a question of the promise and/or the calculation [*calcul*] of another life, replacing and remunerating this one—and not of an irruption opening up this life, in an outside-the-world forming a gaping chasm in this world.

Let us define things carefully here: we speak with some familiarity of "this world" in the sense of this world here, this "down-here," this "mundane" world—but it is a way of speaking that is proper to the West. Whether with the biblical "flesh" or with the Platonic "sensible"—the differences between them being set aside here—the possibility that there should be two "worlds," two regions or regimes of different nature, was given in a particular place (where "this world" is not completely "globalized"). In this place one only knew, or one still only knows, one ensemble to which heaven and earth belong, which is the dwelling of both mankind and gods, regardless of the distance that separates them. "This world" implies that there is another world: another order, another laying out of all things and of life or existence, rather than an "other life" beyond, at the distance of God or of devils. In a certain sense, with "this world" there is no longer any totality of beings or any internal distribution of the regions of the all: or rather, there is such an "all," but it is in itself open, it is at the same time entirely consistent in itself, without outside, and open. The beyond is within [*en-deçà*].

ॐ

It is therefore necessary simultaneously to follow to its last extreme Christianity's movement of self-deconstruction and to reinforce the symmetrical movement of the dis-enclosure of reason. We must not return to the spirit of Christianity, or to the spirit of Europe or of the West. On the contrary, we must refuse every kind of "return," and above all the "return of the religious"—the most threatening of all such returns—and go further into what brought about the invention of this civilization that from now on will be globalized and perhaps lost, that may be approaching its end but is perhaps also capable of another adventure. This invention is a world without God—without any assurance of sense, but without any desire for death.

Doubtless this also means: without Christ and without Socrates. But with what can be found at bottom in both Christ and Socrates, and is more powerful than them: the faculty of being in the world outside of the world, the force and tenderness necessary to salute [*saluer*] another life in the midst of this one. (*To salute*, not to save, that is what is at stake. It is Derrida's "Salut!")[7]

To salute a man other than the son of God—or his double, the son of man, the man of humanism. Another one, yes, opened in the midst of the same, another same man. And another same world. Or even salute an other than man, an other than the world.

But—to salute, here and now. For the outside of the world *in* the world is not "outside" according to the logic of a divorce, a rift, but according to that of an opening that belongs to the world, as the mouth belongs to the body. Better still: the mouth is, or is what makes, the eating and speaking body, just as the other openings are what make it the breathing, listening, seeing, eliminating body. The outside traverses the body in all these ways, and this is how it becomes *a body*: the exposure of a soul. Our bodies are thus entirely, in their turn, openings of the world, and so are other open bodies, those of animals and plants. They can all salute.

Christian Atheism

The possibility of atheism, if by this we mean at least the denial of any kind of afterworld extending this world in order to console it, is inscribed at the source of Christianity, precisely insofar as in itself it is not (only) a religion, or rather insofar as from the outset it had disarranged or destabilized the religion that it was nevertheless creating. This possibility is marked in two ways.

1. On the one hand, Christianity is inaugurated in the affirmation of the presence "down here" of divine otherness or of the other life; not after death, but in death: this is the moment when Lazarus must rise again, now that Christ is rising again. Down here is not a place from which supplications or hopes can be addressed to the beyond. In all its tonalities, adoration is "of here" and opens the *here*—onto no elsewhere.

2. On the other hand, in this affirmation Christianity replays that of philosophy: the death of Socrates is indeed not a passage into another world but the opening of the truth of this world. Where the "world of ideas" was still able to take on a religious hue—and was indeed indicated as the world "of the god" (*ho theos*, a singular that was utterly strange to the Greek ear and that in Plato comes to strike out all the names of the gods along with the entire mythology of their distinct sojourns). This "god" in the singular is only metaphorically elsewhere: it depends on the "right here" [*ici même*] of whoever pronounces it.

In this sense, Socrates and Christ are the same: their deaths open up in the midst of the world, opening the truth of this world as the outside that presents itself right here, an outside that is "divine," if you like, that is in any case "true," that is to say, causing the failure of the indefinite pursuit of any final "sense" that would take place in some paradise or other dwelling of the beyond.[8]

ॐ

There is nothing original about qualifying Christianity as atheist—nor about qualifying Judaism, Islam, and, of course, Buddhism as such (the latter is always described as a "religion without God," though it tends toward a divinization of the Buddha and his avatars). An entire tradition lies behind it, complex in itself and requiring long exposition. A vector of atheism does indeed cut across the great religions, not insofar as they are religious but insofar as they are all contemporary (to speak in very broad terms) with the exit from human sacrifice and with the Western turn in world history, and thus also in philosophy, which is atheism articulated for itself—these religions have witnessed a complete recasting of the "divine," a recasting whose deep driving force pushes toward the removal, if not of the "divine," then at least of "God."

Although this recasting is undeniable and the tradition of atheism or of the becoming-atheist of these religions is well documented, we persistently refuse to know anything about it. Moreover, most of the currently proliferating attempts to reanimate and reevaluate the religious element proceed by ignoring or bypassing this perspective. This is why I feel it is important to emphasize that *only an understanding and an accentuation of Christianity's becoming-atheist* (as well as that of other religions, but I shall say why I am limiting myself to Christianity) *can give us access to a thought that I am indicating as a dis-enclosure of reason.*

I am therefore calling "Christianity" the posture of thought whereby "God" demands to be effaced or to efface himself. Undoubtedly, this definition leaves little room for the contents of the expositions of theological and spiritual truths. However, there is nothing in it that does not originate in such expositions. Nothing—but on the condition that one is able to distill out of doctrine the salt that it carried along in hidden form, even if while dissolving it. And it is indeed a question here of not allowing the *salt of the earth* to become insipid: that is, quite precisely, what gives flavor to this world and to our existence in it: flavor, appreciable quality, a price, value, sense.

God who effaces himself is not only God who takes his leave, as he did of Job, or God who constantly refuses any analogy in this world, as for

Mohammed. It is God who becomes man, abandoning his divinity to the point of plunging it into the mortal condition. Not in order to exit once again from death, but to reveal the immortality in it: very precisely, the immortality *of the dead*. In death, the definitive suspension of sense (of existence) eternally crystallizes the shattering brilliance [*éclat*] of this suspended sense. This does not reduce the pain of dying, even less that of seeing others die. It does not overcome mourning, resolve it as "work" that has been completed: but it does affirm the absolute singularity of the dead.

But the man into whom God "descends" and "empties himself" (Paul's *kenosis*) is not rendered divine by this. On the contrary. God effaces himself in that man: he is this effacement, he is therefore a trace, he is an impalpable, imperceptible vestige of the emptied and abandoned divine. Mankind *is* the abandonment of God: the trace upon him, the trace that he is, constitutes him as a sign of this abandonment. A sign of this: *that the effacement of God is the sense of the world*. The effacement of the Name, of Sense fulfilled. The effacement of the singular name (and even the greatest of these tend to be doomed to effacement; this process is already at work as they become the names of works) contains the effacement of any name claiming to name the Unique (thus the hundredth name of Allah is silent).

Not effacement alone, however. Christianity wants more: not to dwell in the absence of God, in his infinite distance, but to affirm it "among us." That is to say, he is "himself" the *among*: he is the *with* or the *between* of us, this *with* or *between* that we are insofar as *we* are in the proximity that defines the world. The world = all the beings [*étants*] that are near or neighboring one another, that hereby relate to one another, and to nothing else. In this way establishing relations between one another, and to nothing else. "God" was a name for the relation among all beings—therefore, for the *world* in the strongest sense of the word.

In order for this to happen, "God" effaces himself in yet another way: in the *Trinity*. It is a question neither of three gods, nor of a three-headed god. It is exclusively a question of this: God is relation. He is his own relation—which is not a reflexive relation, neither an aseity [*aséité*] nor an ipseity, one that does not relate itself but *relates* absolutely. The ternary structure or appearance goes from one of its aspects to the other via something that is other to each of them, which is the relation *between* them. What is other to each of them is breath, spirit: sense. (That each of the others should be "father" and "son" is not necessarily patriarchal, even though it has been: father and son means one after the other, life and death, proximity and distancing—it is one way among many of saying ourselves all together and as we are, and what's more, not "we" men alone but all "we" beings, we the world, we the world without God).

In a word: the Christian "god" is atheist. In fact, "atheist" signifies the nonpositing of "God," the deposing [*déposition*]⁹ of any god that can be posed as such—that is to say, as a "being" or "subject" to which one property or another is given (including the perfection of all properties): but the Christian "god," insofar as we can name him as such, is not posed, not even self-posed. There is neither a ground nor a space for this: there is neither world nor afterworld, but an opening of sense that produces the spacing of the world and its relation to itself.

It is thus an elsewhere, an outside that opens in the world, or rather opens it to itself, opens it as such, as *world*. But this elsewhere, this outside is here—*hic et nunc*—because it is the excess of this "here" itself over itself, that is to say, over its simple positing. The non-positing of this God is also the non-positing of the world or of beings [*étant*] in general: the world is not posited; it is *given*, given from nothing and for nothing.

Given/nothing or non-given—such is the opposition, and not given/giver, since the latter opposition sends us back toward a giving of the giver itself. As Lévi-Strauss writes: "The fundamental opposition . . . is . . . between being and non-being. A mental effort consubstantial with its history [that of man], and which will cease only with his disappearance from the stage of the universe, compels him to accept the two self-evident and contradictory truths which, through their clash, set his thought in motion."¹⁰ The first motion [*branle*] of thought is that of mythological constructions, which are Lévi-Strauss's concern here. But the aftereffect or *après-coup* of myths that figured oppositions derived from a fundamental opposition (such as heaven and earth, night and day, etc.) leads toward a confrontation with this opposition as such: between the world—in our overdetermination of it in signs, systems, codes, and networks of artifacts—and nothing, a nothing in the provenance of nature and a nothing in the destination of technology. Between the two, our thought is set in motion [*s'ébranle*] once more.

It is important for us to take on this *from nothing and for nothing*: atheism, therefore, as the rigorous consequence and implication of what the Christian West has engendered and extended to the whole world (while dispersing itself in that world and losing its contours in it). A tremendous ambivalence: on the one hand, it can be nihilism; on the other, it can be sense itself, the sense of this—that sense is given outside.

Not Even Atheism

However, it is not enough to understand that Christianity has deployed in this way the possibility of this most daring and elating relation of sense, that which exposes us to the non-positedness of the world and thus to non-entity [*né-ant*]: to what is not [*le non étant*], is not posited, but given, given by no one, by no giver, but is in itself entirely woven from the substance of the gift: gracious, generous, abandoned.

It is not enough to understand that Christianity by itself created its destiny of metamorphosis into atheism—its God having said everything or given everything from the moment that he opened this general deposing or de-positing [*déposition*]. We must understand that this movement goes beyond a metamorphosis. It is not an "ism" converting itself to another "ism."[11] There is neither post-Christianity nor any "renewal" of any sort.

There is not even "atheism"; "atheist" is not enough! It is the positing of the principle that must be emptied. It is not enough to say that God takes leave, withdraws, or is incommensurable. It is even less a question of placing another principle on his throne—Mankind, Reason, Society. It is instead a question of coming to grips with this: the world rests on nothing—and this is its keenest sense.

It is at this point that reason is most conspicuously called into play: atheism consisted essentially in substituting a Reason for a God. In fact, it consisted in substituting a reason—cause, principle, finality—of the world for a god who was himself conceived of as a reason, merely a superior reason, equipped with extraordinary properties of omnipotence and omniscience. The death of this God—and it is only this God who is dead, as Nietzsche says—is nothing other than the death of any Reason endowed with the attributes of necessity and of the completeness of the foundation-production of the totality of beings. This reason did not see that it was putting itself to death in erecting this idol of itself, which was nothing but a God for atheists.

At the same time, in the time of the triumph of this supposed Worldly Reason, the "principle of reason" demanded by Leibniz (everything must have its sufficient reason) came to deploy itself *and* encountered its own uncertainty, trembled on its own foundation.[12] One can even say: the "principle of reason" became an express philosophical demand because the model of rationality that had been constructed was already aware of, or was already touching, its own limit: Did not Newton imply this in his "I feign no hypotheses"—which is to say, I am constructing an order of rational physical laws, but there is no question of using them to provide a reason for [*rendre raison de*] the existence of the world as such?

Kant drew a lesson from this, tracing the circumscription of what he names "understanding" (cognitive reason) and bringing down any imaginable rationality of a "proof of God," which is to say, of an evidencing of the first Reason of the world. From then on, a place was empty. It was occupied by many vicarious instances, for example, Hegelian Reason as a deployment of Spirit. But already with Hegel himself, and even more from his time to ours, what became manifest was that *the empty place must not be occupied*.

Materialisms, positivisms, scientisms, irrationalisms, fascisms or collectivisms, utilitarianisms, individualisms, historicisms, legalisms, and even democratisms, without mentioning all the relativisms, skepticisms, logicisms—all duly atheist—will have been attempts, more or less pitiful or frightening, to occupy this place, with greater or lesser dissimulation of the effort to do so, for one had, after all, become somewhat aware that this was not what needed to be done.

Such is still, and on a renewed basis, our responsibility: to keep the place empty, or better still, perhaps, to ensure that there shall be no more place for an instance or for a question of a "reason given" [*"raison rendue"*], of foundation, origin, and end. *Let there be no more place for God—and in this way, let an opening, which we can discuss elsewhere whether to call "divine," open.*

Israel—Islam

Having thus drawn Christianity out of itself and even beyond atheism, I may have given the impression that, though I have noted some converging traits in the two other Western monotheisms, I am placing them at a lesser level of power or interest in the enterprise that concerns me.

On the one hand, I hold—as should be obvious—that this triple monotheism, in its profound and secret unity, carries the certainty, paradoxical for a religion, that I have just formulated: "The world rests on nothing." No pillars, no turtle, no ocean, not even an abyss or yawning gulf: for the world is the gulf that swallows every type of backworld. The world is strangeness itself, absolute strangeness: the strangeness of the real, the quite tangible reality of this anomaly or of this exception devoid of all attachment. Each god says this in his own way: he says "Listen!" or he says "Love!" or he says "Read!" Of course, this extreme triple contradiction does not claim to sum up anything: it merely suggests that these three gods neither posit nor found, but essentially do something else. This triple God is not, first of all, he who made the world (and in any case, he makes it from nothing, which is to say without foundation or material: he does not make the world, he makes *there be* a world), rather he is first of all, or even uniquely, he who addresses. He is the one who calls, who interpellates. He is a god of speech. Without entering further here into the implications of this formula, I will limit myself to saying: the nature and law of language is to be addressed, both well on the hither side and far beyond all signification. Adoration responds to this address, or rather, resonates with it.

On the other hand, and to the contrary, I hold that, of the three religions, only one has undone itself as a religion and has in some way transformed itself into an irrigation system for the culture of the modern world (its morals, its law, its humanism, and its nihilism). We must say it precisely, though I cannot linger on this point—only one of the veins of Christianity flowed in this direction. This was the Reformation and the part of Catholicism that took inspiration from it, as well as at least a part of Christian mysticism (particularly Eckhart) but not Catholicism *stricto sensu*, no more than the Orthodox churches. This is to say not only that the Christianity that I claim is deconstructing itself and entering into a relation of mutual dis-enclosure with modern reason is far from being one with the ensemble of dogmas, institutions, and sociopolitical behavior of the different churches, but that it even breaks with them. This break is not new; it doubtless opens from the beginning of Christianity (e.g., between James and Paul, but perhaps also in Paul himself, or else in the difference between John and the Synoptic Gospels), and it can be found down the ages (Anselm, Eckhart, Francis of Assisi, Fénelon, and, of course, the great Reformers up to Barth, Bultmann, and Benhoeffer; more subtly, it traverses Augustine or Pascal—and these are only a few names at random). I do not wish to linger here: I only wish to emphasize that it is not the entirety of the Christian religion that is dis-enclosing itself, outside religion and outside Christianity. Not even, and in some way, the entirety of the reformed confessions, as certain conflicts (particularly around homosexuality) have shown. But the presence of this disposition is proper to Christianity, to what under the name of "Christendom" for a time structured what one could already have named "Europe," with its knowledge, its law, its expansion, its humanism, its art.

∽

But comparison with the two other monotheisms is what interests us here. In a way, and starting with the least obvious thing, insofar as we are considering Judaism and Islam as religions, the disposition which I have just declared proper to Christianity is also present in the two other confessions. Doubtless each of them possesses a vein exceeding religion, that is to say, a vein that dissipates observance in adoration. More than one mystic from each tradition confirms this for us.

However, the Jewish and the Muslim religions remain religions, very rich and complex systems of representation and observance, and it is difficult to see how they could be "secularized" (whatever the precise concept of the word might be). This is because they have no reason to enter into tension or conflict with institutions comparable to those of Christian Churches. The absence of such "Churches" obviously plays an important role here, one that has often been commented upon. But there is a reason for this absence: Christianity hastened to build a Church—to conceive of itself as a Church—because from the beginning it understood itself as an "assembly" (this is the meaning of the word) distinct de jure from any other assembly in the world, and therefore first of all political or sociopolitical.

It is starting from this point that it seems to me most possible to elucidate the relations among the three monotheisms—of course, in two rigorously different ways.

First of all, the relation between Christianity and Judaism. If one does not forget that Christianity is Judeo-Christian by birth—and in a sense, as we shall see, does not cease to be that—then one must remember that the Jewish currents in which it was born were tending toward a radical difference between "kingdoms." Judaism was undergoing the experience—which, in truth, began in it long ago—of a separation between kingdoms, that is, an experience of the "not of this world" in the midst of the world.[13] On the one hand, this experience takes the Christian form that will become, in a few centuries, the ambiguous, eminently debatable form in which a Church that is quite distinct from any Kingdom or Empire will nonetheless mix up its destiny in a thousand ways with those of kingdoms and empires, at times (often) to the point of apostasizing itself by becoming a power in the world.[14] On the other hand, it takes the form of the dispersion of Israel, a *diaspora* that is precisely the carrying of this affirmation of the separateness of "kingdoms" into any possible place, whether kingdom or empire. (It is remarkable that, in certain respects, Paul should be the one who, on the one hand, suppresses the difference between Jews, Greeks, and "nations" in general, who is so strongly opposed to those who wish to withdraw into small formations that historians call "Judeo-Christian," and, on the other hand, who emphasizes in so many ways the congenital Judaism of Christianity, if only because he speaks of a "circumcision of the heart." With him perhaps emerges the first condition of possibility for what will much later provoke the Christian hatred of Jews, which I shall attempt to characterize as a form of self-hatred.)

Much later still, in a history that has been transformed, "Zionism" will be invented and, after it, what led to the State of Israel as we know it. I will not enter into this history: I merely note that it originates at least to a large degree in the exacerbation of what one names "antisemitism."

What is antisemitism (extremely poorly named, since Arabs are Semites)? I hazard the following hypothesis: it is the hatred of Jews developed by Christians, for whom they represent an upholding of the distinction between the kingdoms, from which the Catholic, Reformed, and Orthodox Churches have constantly departed.[15] The Jew is the witness to what Christianity, in this respect, ought to be, and this respect is not indifferent, or a detail of theology, because it engages nothing less than the confusion, sometimes of the most hypocritical sort, between spiritual testimony and sociopolitical domination. The hatred of Jews is a hatred because it proceeds from a conscience that feels guilty about *itself*, and this hatred attempts to destroy the testimony to what Christians have a duty to be. This is also why, as history could show, the Christians who were least touched by games of power were also the least antisemitic. (What the hatred of Jews becomes with Nazism is not Christian in principle, although many did find precedents in the existing tradition. Yet Nazism is the affirmation par excellence of an unique and exclusive *Reich*: it does not wish to and cannot know anything of another "kingdom" opened in the midst of the world.)

It is not as a religion that Judaism provoked the hatred of Christians: it is insofar as this religion, but also at times a Jewish thought entirely withdrawn from religion, represents what Christians were all too aware of—and all too ready to deny—that they had developed from a Judaism becoming detached from the kingdom of Israel, a Judaism that was deconstructing itself.[16]

༄

The case of Islam is obviously quite different. It came after Christianity, in a context where the latter could only appear completely linked to Empire—to the two Empires of the West and the East.[17] Thus from the beginning Islam took on a political as well as a religious figure, and the great division between Sunni and Shi'a itself proceeds from a political struggle, which removes nothing from the importance of their doctrinal differences. Still, the question of the caliphate, and of the distinction between a political power and a religious authority (never for its part taking on the form of a Church), has been posed more than once and in several ways. But this is not a subject I can properly address.[18]

One must remark, however, that Islam implies, in a highly singular way, the coexistence of an intrication of and a distinction between the profane and religious orders. On the one hand, everything is under the attentive gaze of God; on the other, his absolute incommensurability demands nothing of the believer other than to affirm it according to the forms prescribed to him, without mixing it with worldly affairs in any way. There is, in sum, neither one nor two kingdoms: there is the register of human affairs and that of the unique affair of the believer as such, which is to confess the "All-Powerful, Merciful."

In a sense, Islam is dedicated to adoration, even as it deploys an empire. This is why Christendom ended up wanting to repel this empire, as a rival to the one it was beginning once again to develop. But even if this relation of political force was accompanied by the accusation of being "infidel" and by large-scale confrontations, never have Christians hated Muslims. The former did not see in the latter a mirror of their own malfeasance. On the contrary, the Christians who are most disengaged from the Churches can without difficulty recognize the proximity of their traditions to those of the great Muslim Sufis, like Ibn Arabi, or those of the mystics like Al-Hallaj.

Some Sufis have even gone so far as to declare that nothing exists except God. Such an affirmation—seemingly quite Spinozist—obviously does not signify that only a unique "One" exists, which, resting only on itself, could also only collapse into itself, but on the contrary that everything only *is* in and according to its relation to what or who is thus named, to this unnamable incommensurable who or which is not, for his or its part (but he or it has no "part" that is apart) an existent, but rather the measurelessness of existing.

It remains that, for reasons different from those in the case of Judaism, but also in conditions quite other than those of the kingdoms, empires, or sultanates of long ago, Islam today forms states founded on a reference to religion. I shall not venture into this territory. One cannot, however, avoid remarking that, in a world that has emerged from a major transformation in the very midst of which there is at play what I have designated in the Christian mode as the "difference between kingdoms," now understood as the opening of the world onto its own absence of a world beyond and as the necessary dis-enclosure of its reason—in such a world, one cannot be content with what until now has appeared self-evident regarding the relations between "religion" and "politics," whether they be relations of exclusion or inclusion. Everything in this regard will have to be reworked.

One World, Two Dimensions

I do not wish to take these suggestions any further, so I will stop with this. On the one hand, (Judeo-)Christianity—and, to a degree, Islam too—has deconstructed itself in a culture of science, democracy, and the rights and the emancipation of mankind. But along the way it has never stopped making the identity of the "mankind" in question more opaque or more slippery; this could, in fact, mean that (Judeo-)Christianity asks whether it is not from itself that it should deliver itself. On the other hand, triple monotheism—which is to say, this profound shock to the religious order or to the relation to the sacred, to the ground of sacrality itself—has disenclosed itself by telling us that Reason cannot be satisfied with explanations or "reasons given" [*raisons rendues*] but pushes toward an incommensurable and an unnamable of sense—or toward a truth without concept or figure. If it fails to give this push or drive its due, reason wilts and sinks into general commensurability and an interminable nomination in which all names are interchangeable.

What remains of religion—Jewish, Christian, Muslim—can now only provide a formal testimony for this drive (which I am naming adoration). (I say nothing about the world's other religious forms, those from Asia and Africa in particular. At times, some people evoke them as possible modes of recourse by invoking forms of meditation and mental exercise or spiritual practice: they forget that one cannot easily transplant cultural elements and that, for many reasons, we are not capable of reflecting on the possible or impossible relations such forms might assume with modern rationality. This is because in Asia, Africa, or Oceania either they have already been transformed or contact with the rationality that came from the "West" is still not, for certain portions of the population, sufficiently pronounced to allow us to judge.)

This is why my interest is not in gathering together some sort of remainder, neither of Christianity nor of the entire Western monotheist complex. It is in understanding how the civilization that propagated itself throughout the world in the forms of scientific, legal, and moral rationality has arrived at a sort of confinement both of reason and of the world that makes us despair of ourselves. For we know that this confinement is contrary to the drive—to the pressure, the impetus, or, why not, the instinct—that searches, in us, for contact with the "open": because this open, we ourselves are it, language is it, the world itself is it.

(Saying "the open" is already an abuse of language. One ought to avoid this substantive as well as what pulls it toward either a concept or a name. It [*ça*] opens up precisely at a distance from both.)

An open world is a world without myths and without idols, a world without religion if we understand by this word the observance of behaviors and representations that respond to a claim for sense as a claim for assurance, destination, accomplishment. This does not mean that in what one calls "the religions" it should be a question only of myths and idols, nor that it should be easy to decide what is and what is not "myth" and "idol" in the critical sense of these words (senses that were decided, we must remember, in the send-off or *coup d'envoi* of Western history, between the Greeks and the Jews). At the very least, it is possible to say that what constitutes the myth and the idol in these senses has to do with the assurance that each one—the mythical tale [*récit*] or the figure as idol—assures a presence and responds to a demand. In other words, it "gives reasons for [*rend raison de*] existence. In a paradoxical way, it is in its desire to "rationalize," to provide a ground or account, to "give reasons" that religion can exhaust itself, becoming nothing more than mythology and idolatry. On the contrary, it can exhaust myths and idols—and it can do so in itself—from the moment when it no longer seeks to give reasons, or no longer claims to do so.

But this is just as much the affair of Reason itself—that of this pressure or drive (Kant's *Trieb*), directed toward the "unconditioned" or toward the unlocalizable outside of the world, in the world itself.

For this reason, the separation of the "kingdoms" or the "worlds" is decisive here.[19] It is not that one must be subordinated to the other—which would still be for one to reign over the other—nor is it that their reigning powers should be in opposition, which would put them in the condition of kingdoms "of this world." Rather, they are to each other as vertical is to horizontal: heterogeneous, heterotopic dimensions, which cross at one point. This point, lacking dimension as do all points, forms the opening of the world, the opening of sense in the world. Through this opening, sense penetrates and escapes at the same time, in the same movement and in "making sense" just as much by the penetration as by the escape.

This opening is nothing other than the gaping that has been characterized as an "immense fracture" between a high and a low but that is equally at the common root of Western monotheism, what one can designate as "the prophecy of Abraham," which represents "a new conception of heritage and of history, a new filiation, a new definition of land and of blood." For "the land of all the nations shall be the promised land for the sons of Abraham. A land without land, however, without divisible, assignable territories, without countries, without nations. It is a desert land where a son of Abraham can be born from every rock."[20]

That from every rock could be born one who inherits the promise that promises nothing but this dis-enclosure of the territory and of all circumscription of sense, this is what the opening I am speaking of signifies—far beyond any religious or philosophical representation or conception.

To avoid misunderstanding, we must also emphasize that the point of sense does indeed belong to the world, to "this world here," just as the rock belongs to the desert and the point of intersection belongs to the horizontal as much as to the vertical line. Being in the world without being of the world—this condition that a certain Christian monarchism sought to incarnate—is not to live in the world while abstaining from it, holding oneself in some retreat, even if entirely "interior" and "spiritual." It is to think and feel the world according to its opening. Which is to say, first of all, according to an irreducibility to all relations defined by a common measure of forces and values. But it is to think a value and a force that are incommensurable, and consequently also to think an unfigurable form.

"A" force, "a" value—yes, in the sense that the monotheisms introduced the "one" not as a numerical index but rather as something external to all numeration, to any counting. This "one" embraces the multiple without unifying it. Its unity lies in the fact that it is essentially withdrawn from all that can posit equivalences—between beings, between forces, between forms. It is precisely the sort of unity that is that of *everyone* [chacun]: of each singular, whether one understands this as a "subject" or as any kind of discernable singularity, the leaf of a tree or the crest of a wave.[21]

With

Perhaps it is not impossible to bring together and focus the stakes by saying this: what has prevailed in triple monotheism, and in its finally "globalized" expression (which is to say, in the strong sense: what has been driven out of its birthplace to the point of both traversing the world and making itself a world, to the point of making itself the new age of the world and therefore of man) is the thought of a "God" who is *with* and not beyond or above. That God is with us is doubtless the most profoundly shared and constant thought of triple monotheism. It ultimately says this: that in the decomposition of his religious figures, above all of the Christian figure that opened this dissolution, "God" is nothing other—if we are dealing with a thing at all, and it is perhaps *the thing* itself—than this *with* itself.

There once were "gods and mankind," then there was "God with us," there is henceforth "we with ourselves [*entre nous*]"—and to say it once again, this "we" becomes the pronoun of all beings, allowing what "mankind" is or does in the bosom of this universal coexistence to appear in a new—uncertain, disquieting—light. There is no "secularization" in this narrative, but instead transformations of the world's being world, which is not something given once and for all, but which replays and relaunches the ex nihilo that is its sharing [*partage*].

This is what must be understood in the motif of "revelation." The so-called "revealed" religions distinguished themselves from others only in this way: the sign of the infinite, which is itself infinite, sends itself of itself [*s'envoie*]. It is certain that all religions are traversed by a motion, an impetus of this sort. All religions and ultimately all kinds of knowledge, science, or philosophy: for we could not even be within the movement of any knowing whatsoever if the desire for the infinite did not thrust us there. Finite knowledge is a kind of information, an instruction; it is not what opens itself to the inexhaustible bottom of things. If we are "finite" insofar as we are mortal, this finitude configures our access to the infinite. There are or there have been mythological, shamanical, esoteric, metaphysical, and gnostic versions of this configuration, as well as others. What "revelation" introduces is ultimately a disconfiguration. Revelation is not a doctrine. What is revealed is not concerned with content-based principles, articles of faith, and revelation does not unveil anything that is hidden: it reveals insofar as it addresses, and this address constitutes what is revealed. God calls Abraham, Mary, Mohammed. The call calls for a response, which is another call. It is not a question of learning a doctrinal corpus, but of responding. Call and response (which also means: the responsibility to respond) of all to all, of everyone to everyone, as if only to salute one another: nothing more, nothing less, but in this way clearing endless paths [*voies*] and voices [*voix*] between fortuitous existences.

Truth revealed is truth that contains no doctrine or preaching. It is not the truth of any adequation or unveiling. It is the simple, infinite truth of the suspension of sense: an interruption, for sense cannot be completed, and an overflowing, for it does not cease.

This is also why our world is the world of literature: what this term designates in a dangerously insufficient, decorative, and idle way is nothing other than the opening of the voices of the "with." On the same site where what we call myth gave voice to the origin, literature tunes in to the innumerable voices of our sharing [*partage*]. We share the withdrawal of the origin, and literature speaks starting from the interruption of myth

and in some way in that interruption: it is in that interruption that literature makes it possible for us to make sense.[22] This sense is the sense of
fiction: that is to say, neither mythical nor scientific, but giving itself in
creation, in the fashioning (*fingo*, *fictum*) of forms that are themselves
mobile, plastic, ductile, and according to which the "with" configures itself indefinitely.

What we must say about literature in this way is valid for all that constitutes "art," all the irreducibly plural—singular/plural—ways of fashioning and exchanging sense outside of signification (for even the art of
language and literary fiction do not signify: they carry significations away
into another realm, where signs refer [*renvoient*] to the infinite).

꒰

By way of a final cadence:

> Who knows who she was, his model that day: a woman from the
> street? the wife of a patron? The atmosphere in the studio electric,
> but with what? Erotic energy? The penises of all those men, their
> *verges*, tingling? Undoubtedly. Yet something else in the air too. Ad-
> oration. The brush pauses as they adore the mystery that is mani-
> fested to them: from the body of the woman, life flowing in a
> stream.[23]

Mysteries and Virtues

> The destruction of an illusion does not yield any truth, only *a little more ignorance*.[1]

1

The dis-enclosure of reason is the effect, or rather the remainder, of deconstructed Christianity, of religion's having withdrawn from itself, pushed off from its observances and beliefs. Reason has moved away from the wish to give reasons [*rendre raison*]. Or rather, it knows that "giving a reason" goes beyond any reason that can be given. It knows that giving one's reasons is an interminable process: one chases after the inexplicable and the unjustifiable, the fortuitous and the evil.

These last two are linked, for in one way or another evil always consists in refusing contingency. Evil introduces a necessity. If evil begins with murder, that is because a necessity emerges in murder: "You must cease to be!" The opposite is not—necessarily—"you must be," but rather: we are ourselves the relation among all beings; this is how things are; this might not have come to be. But it did come to be, and there also came to be a sign according to which we are for one another and by one another. A sign according to which we are signs for one another, "we," all the beings of the world.

Such a sign does not issue from necessity. Just like the coming about of all existences and their encounters, it is fortuitous. It is a sign of this contingency. It is a gaze, a gesture, a contact, a sonority. It is the fact that the animal, the vegetable, and the mineral signify to one another, not to mention the living and the inanimate, the speaking and the mute, the constructed and the spontaneous, the machine and the organ, one sex and the other, youth and old age, one language and another, one sense and another, and so on. Between these poles or points of reference, among which none is simply identical to itself or strictly consists in itself, circulate a polymorphous echoing and referring [*renvoi*] and a profusion of signs of contingency: the touching-one-another-together of this encounter through which there is a world and existence in the world.

This proliferating, unordered, overabundant signification forms the effect or rather the remainder of Christian "creation" and "salvation": the effect or rather the remainder of the extreme withdrawal of "god" that forms the ground of "monotheism." The same is true of the dis-enclosure of reason that opens onto the extreme withdrawal of any "given reason." In other words, onto the extreme withdrawal of what we most often think we designate when speaking of "sense," the sense of life or the sense of the world.

༜

This dis-enclosure cannot be identified as a secularization. Indeed, in a way it is the opposite of one. Here "secularization" means a process supposed to convert religious values, rules, and configurations into secular values, rules, or configurations (whether lay or worldly, as you will: symptomatically, we lack any terms to describe our world save those taken from the religious lexicon). But as one knows, although the fact is constantly forgotten in hasty usages of the word *secularization*, nothing is less clear than the precise sense of the "conversion" that takes place in this way. The word *conversion*, here used deliberately to borrow once again from the religious lexicon, is itself only one of the possible terms for describing the terrain of this problem: Does it involve a metaphorical transferal? An analogical one? Is it merely a transposition of form, or also of content? And most of all, how are any of these terms to be understood? Let us take the most striking example of this phenomenon, that of the political secularization of divine sovereignty (as posed by Carl Schmitt). It is immediately obvious that the sovereign power of a State or within a State can only be thought as the transposition of a divine power by asking whether and how it is possible to convert the absolutely originary power of a god anterior to any law (or only obeying his own "law," if one prefers to put it that way) into the power to decide on the exception in relation to a given law, which will itself have allowed for the possibility of such a decision. In moving from the first to the second register, everything is displaced, however insignificant this displacement might appear. The same is true when one says that the utopias, projections, or historical projects of various forms of "socialism" will have amounted to secularized messianisms, because in order to give this "secularization" a consistent content, the supposedly "worldly" messianisms must not be deprived of what is proper to religious messianism: the impossibility of designating the Messiah, his presence or absence, and what's more, the necessity of believing at once that he has already come and that he will be always to come.

The idea of "secularization" is based on an optical illusion: the culture of the "century" only superficially adopts some aspects of the culture of the "beyond." The latter is of another order, and profoundly so. In fact, what I am naming here "the culture of the beyond" relies on the dissociation of the two orders; it can open up only within the other order as strangeness and heterogeneity. This is why the thought of secularization in fact presupposes the reverse of what it proposes: it has already preinterpreted the world of the beyond in terms of this world, for instance, by representing God as a King. This mistake is present in the discourse of religion itself when it speaks of two kingdoms: but henceforth we must learn that the "other kingdom" is no kingdom, that it cannot be conceived according to the parameters of power, principles, authority, jurisdiction, and so on.

Religion doubtless always knew this, more or less confusedly: this knowledge surfaces here and there in spirituality and in mysticism. It can also be found via what can pass for the most esoteric dogma: I shall come to this presently. But it falls to us today to free up this knowledge as much as possible in order to give it its true reach, which is no more religious than it is, strictly speaking, philosophical: it is the knowledge of human experience, the knowledge of mankind alone insofar as it "infinitely surpasses mankind" or as it "ek-sists," insofar as it is a "dancer above the abyss." It does not involve secularizing, converting, or transposing, but rather opening ourselves up to what bears us, what pushes us, what stems from what, for man, is the experience that is the most profound, most deeply buried, and yet most to come: man insofar as he has engendered himself as "modern." For "modern" has always meant: that for which nothing is given, not even itself.

2

The title of this chapter, "Mysteries and Virtues," resounds in a particularly religious and even pious way. I am merely borrowing these terms from Christian theology and spirituality, but here I can propose a transcription of them that reveals what lies behind this borrowing. The title would then become: "Flashes [*Éclairs*] and Drives."

Mystery, as we understand it in the wake of Christianity, does not designate a hidden, secret reality, buried in the arcana of an impenetrable divine knowledge. In truth, the word retains something of its Greek usage, where it corresponded to the final stage of an initiation into a "religion of mysteries": to the revelation of an object or a sentence to which the initiate was permitted access only on completion of her journey.[2] The revelation of Christian mystery is not the unveiling of some secret: on the contrary, it reveals what reveals itself on its own, what does nothing other than reveal itself. It is a flash revealing forms and presences that, rather than being hidden in the night, are simply available for the light to come and make visible [*éclairer*].

The irruption of light is neither authorized nor obtained through an initiatory procedure: light opens its eyes on mystery, which of itself allows itself to be seen, and which is in fact nothing other than light itself.

This also means that light opens the eyes of someone (of "mankind") or that it opens its own eyes: for light is a gaze as well as a clarity, and the gaze is light. In this context, vision is not the relation of a seeing subject to the forms of visible objects, it is—as in the moment of awakening, before the distinction of forms and distances—the clarification of a presence. A "worldly presence," as we have come to say, but that must not be understood as the conjunction of some being with a world that would lie outside it: the world is simply the presence of all those who are present. Light, the way in which this presence presents itself to itself, signals and salutes itself.

A sudden, instantaneous, brief light—always appearing suddenly in the night. A "flash" therefore, less in the sense of a dazzling than in that of fleeting clarity, of a spark. It is not the blaze of apocalypse but the renewal of dawn.[3]

It is as if this mystery were obvious [*l'évidence*]: one cannot *not* see it, and doubtless in a sense we all see it, even if not everyone looks out for it or pays attention to it. The flash of mystery is not ultimately of a nature different from the sudden appearance of the *fiat lux*, which is to say, the separation of light from darkness whereby a world begins. In the same way, the "divine" does not refer to anything but this separation between day (*dies, divus*) and night. The opening of the world is the first mystery, and doubtless the only one, or the one that contains all others. The world is the obvious [*évidence*] itself, and not only the obviousness of what comes before my eyes, but that whereby my eyes and the world open themselves together, the former included within the latter, which, at the same time, penetrates them.

Separation, distinction, opening—relation. We shall learn to discern how mystery is the mystery of relation.

For now, let us simply read what Pasolini has to say: "everything was contained in him, everything that was needed for love. And nothing closed, nothing unexpressed, obscured: his mystery like his gaze was resplendent with clarity."[4]

☞

As for the virtues, let us first say that we shall consider only those that theology names "theologal," which is to say, those concerning the relation to God. There are three: faith, hope, and charity. Before looking at them, we should recall what the word *virtue* bears within it, not only in its Latin etymology—*virtus*, virile quality[5]—but also in all the signification that has remained attached to it, even though a certain moral—and moralistic—representation tends to cover it over. Often "virtue" is taken to mean a disposition that conforms to some contrastive distribution into "virtues" and "vices," which is to say, a fixed definition of "good" and "evil." Being "virtuous," as used to be expected of a "pure" young girl or as is today of a "good" trader, consists in respecting values and norms that one is able to define. Even if one does not worry about searching after ultimate justifications, such definable values and norms are offered at times by a given state of mores, at others, by a demand to be prudent, balanced, wise.

This valuation [*valeur*] of the word entirely neglects the sense of *force* that is above all at work in *virtus*, a sense that we still recognize when we use an expression like the "relaxing virtues of a lullaby." Virtue is above all vigor, a force straining toward . . . and capable of . . . : it is no accident that themes such as efficiency and even productivity recover this value for us. Here a term for an aim is substituted for the energy of aiming; a parallel substitution can be seen in the word *valeur* [meaning both "value" and valor"], in which what made the *valeur* of the "valorous" [*valeureux*] close to bravery has disappeared. The same thing is happening: instead of value [*valeur*] being brought back to the vigor of an affirmation that proves its value or worth [*se fait valoir*], or that constitutes the value of some plan, enterprise, or gesture, it is considered as being deposited in a repository [*banque*] of givens (e.g., "social justice" or, in a more complex way, "democracy"). In the same way, instead of virtue designating vigor, ardor turned toward an affirmation whose content cannot be separated from this very ardor, it names an available and determined content (thus one can speak of "the virtue of a citizen" without imagining that the *virtus* of the citizen could create a tension in the city via a demand for revolt and rupture).

"Virtue" is the impetus carried along, impelled or thrust onward, by a "value" that is not simply an available and determined "good" but that is valuable to the degree that this thrust carries one beyond what has been or could be determined. We shall not speak of the virtue of someone who accomplishes impeccably a task assigned to him, but we shall use the term for whoever takes "impeccable" to be a limited notion and who wishes for more, who longs to go further, who commits himself to a hyperbole of "value." That is not limited to an item of work; it desires more than work, it wants to go to the impossible. One can imagine this movement equally well in the carrying out of a domestic or a professional task, in a commitment within the bonds of sociability, friendship, or love, in the carrying out of art or sport: everywhere there is, on the one hand, an order of impeccable accomplishment and, on the other, a going beyond that is de jure limitless, the order of a thrust that is infinite. We know full well how this thrust is indissociable from what we call "love," "sport," "art," or "thought," but we also know that in these registers an element of the impeccable and the satisfying can be established. We also know that the infinite thrust can become obsessive compulsion, perfectionism, mania: everything can be deformed and confined as an illness, but compulsion is not drive [*pulsion*].

For that is what we must name. We must say that virtue is above all *drive*. Because of the French translation of the Freudian *Trieb*, we have become accustomed to understanding drive as an obscure, uncontrollable, wild, and definitively threatening thrust. It is true that it is so: but this is because it appears where force(s) precede and follow us, where forces are not concerned with a subject's calculation and projection but where one might rather say that a subject, by welcoming these forces, by espousing their impetus, might have some chance of shaping itself (at least, if one thinks that a "subject" should be "shaped"; we can also say: if one thinks that man is to have any chance of "infinitely surpassing man").

This is why the *Trieb* is also the thrust internal to reason that Kant designates as the movement of reason toward the "unconditioned" (or the "undetermined," *das Unbestimmte*). Kant is the first to attempt to give this drive its due, namely, a due exceeding the order of the "understanding" and knowledge of an object, a due that is regulated by nothing other than an opening to the infinite. Since the Kantian operation, thought has constantly been in relation to this opening, and Freud himself felt that, in discussing drive, he was touching on this: on what, in the psyche, infinitely surpasses any psychology. This is why he said "the drives are our myths," meaning both, on the one hand, that they are not observable physical forces and, on the other, that they index our condition of being thrown, thrust, propelled without origin or end in a movement that arrives at no "sense"—neither of life, of death, of civilization, nor of love. In speaking of the "doctrine of the drives" as "our mythology," Freud distances himself from every philosophy and more generally from every "doctrine," just as he would like his "metapsychology" to be distanced from every metaphysics and from every psychology. But of course he does not do this in order to move toward a religion: it is a premonition of a way of considering existence and the world differently from any assignation of knowledge and representation.[6] After Kant, Hegel, and Nietzsche, at the same time as Heidegger, Freud in his own way thinks a dis-enclosure of reason, and he thinks it expressly under the name of "drive": the virtue of the relation to what can be accomplished by neither knowledge nor representation—and therefore by neither "sense" nor "truth," according to one of those regimes.

The main consequence is ontological, or at least one that dis-encloses ontology: thrust is not first of all the relation of a "subject" to some "object"—it is in principle beyond the "object"—but it is the condition or nature of "being." "Being," understood as a verb, *to be*, means "to thrust or push" (or "to impel," "to throw," and even "to shake," "to excite"). Being, to be, is drive [*pulsion*] and beating [*pulsation*] of the being in general. The drive of reason is its desire for the thing itself.

3

The essential mysteries, that is, those whose proper concern is "God," are three: the trinity, the incarnation, and the resurrection. The link among them defines nothing other than the considerable—atheological—displacement that the thinking of "God" undergoes.

This displacement proceeds from an experience, an awaiting, and a disposition that stem from much further back than "religion," than any religious filiation or transmission—and displacement is already, in this sense, initiated by Judaism. This is why it later leads toward an "exit from religion." One could put it this way: the gods have always been the advocates or representatives of humans' relation to the enigma that they are for themselves and, through this first enigma, to the enigma that the world in itself is. Whether one says enigma, question, or putting into play, what matters is destination to and by another dimension, one that is heterogeneous and exorbitant: that of "sense" insofar as it is a reference to [*renvoi à*] another, works free from, shakes off and tosses aside, or throws away any consistency of "being." The gods are born together with man and from him in order to designate what Heidegger's formulation says, namely, that "the existent is a being for whom, in its being, being is in question." The gods name the inequality or the inequivalence of being to itself, or its difference and its *différance*. (Once again, *dies/divus*, the difference between day and night.) They name it or signal it. The relation to the gods is a relation to this difference or, more precisely, a relation of mankind to itself (and through it, of the world to itself) according to its *différance*.

The first form of this relation is sacrifice: the "sacred" being the name of the heterogeneous, of the specific modes of conduct that threw out a bridge toward it. Their matrix and model is the act of putting a man to death, that is, his consacration, whereby other men in their turn communicate with the sacred. The progressive disappearance of human sacrifice in all of the Eastern Mediterranean, even if animal and plant sacrifices persisted for a long time afterward, represented the turning point whereby, at the same time as a civilization turned around (thanks to iron, writing, trade, detachment from the rural and the imperial), the relation to the gods underwent a metamorphosis. Where before the relation to their sacred presences prevailed, various forms of the relation between men begin to prevail: the deployment of exchanges in multiple ways, the formation of autonomous "cities" or "peoples," defined by what they share [*leurs partages*] and by their own constitutions rather than by any belonging to a sacred heritage. This is the world of *greekjew, jewgreek* with which the history of our world opens up. Religion, its avatars, and even its metamorphosis and exit from itself all depend on the movement of culture or civilization. This is why deconstructing Christianity comes down to a close scrutiny of this movement and, correlatively, to disenclosing the reason that this movement produced.[7]

In this new world, where the relations of men among themselves gradually take over from the common or collective relation to divine powers, relation itself somehow comes to occupy the place of the sacred. Already the God of Israel is one of a "covenant," a formula unknown to any other religion. Mohammed's God will be one of an address and a convocation that calls for nothing other than for this call to be honored. Relation becomes pregnant in these two forms. The mystery of the trinity articulates

"God" himself as relation. That is to say, it removes from him the property of "being" in the sense of a being [*être*] or being [*étant*] that is consistent in itself, of a subject that can be represented as a person or even as any "entity" whatsoever.

The divine trinity does not mean that God is divided into three, nor that he forms the union of the three. The generation of the son by the father should not be understood as a descendance but according to their identity of nature, within which opens up the possibility of "relation" as such, the "relation" that is an echoing and referring [*renvoi*] of sense from one to the other. This is how the son can be said to be "begotten, not made": he is not exterior to the father but somehow opens in him the relational dimension. This dimension in its turn is called spirit.[8] Spirit is relation, or sense, according to which subjects, which do not exist independently of relation, are able to present themselves to one another. Or rather, relation is the non-being according to which beings can make sense, beings that therefore cannot subsist outside this non-being.

Sacrifice had been the form of the relation with an elsewhere or an outside whose sacred presences—the gods—were themselves caught up in a larger outside, which was named destiny, necessity, night, or primordial abyss. There was no relation with this outside. At most the gods were able to offer some form of mediation, but it was fragile and uncertain. Tragedy thus presented the possibility of somehow playing—setting into play by setting the scene [*mettant en scène*]—the impossibility of relation to this outside by making this very impossibility a type of relation. Tragedy has always appeared to be a heritage that we are incapable of truly appropriating because in certain respects it continues to draw on cult and ritual. On the one hand, it looks backward toward myth, and on the other, it is inscribed in what we can call a civil religion. A civil religion would be a relation among men, men who recognize themselves in its terms, between the autonomy of law and the indigenous nature [*autochtonie*] of the city. But the history of Antiquity—which is to say, the history of the anthropological mutation that we have inherited—is the history of the repeated failure of civil religions. The problems of democracy and the republic are born there and come down to us, at the same time as the inverse disposition appears there, namely, that which separates orders, kingdoms, and cities between "heaven" and "earth."

What did not take place as civil religion—as the autonomous, self-enclosed sense of a human ("too human"?) world—comes about in the configuration, at once conjunctive and disjunctive, of a world order that takes its legitimacy from itself and from an opening in the midst of the world, an opening turned toward an outside that is not another world but what, in the bosom of the world, remains an excess. This excess is the "sense" of or in the relation among all the beings that make up, that *are* this world, and that "have" nothing but it, lacking the power of the Outside (destiny, night, abyss). The entire outside thus flows back into the world and this outgoing tide opens within the world the breach of a henceforth problematic, enigmatic, *mysterious* "sense."

The mystery of the trinity strikes this spark: sense is relation itself, the outside of the world is therefore within the world without being of the world.

4

The two other mysteries proceed from this. This "god" who has already in himself renounced his being also renounces the separation of his divinity from mankind in order that it be "made flesh"; espousing the mortal character of this flesh, he opens up within death another life, an eternal life. "Incarnation" and "resurrection" are not and cannot be prodigious and, strictly speaking, incredible fables. What remains of them, what belongs to us or comes back to us, is the task of newly understanding their provenance and their destination: they come from the region of history where human culture grasps itself as a "world" in a sense detached from any cosmogony and where the ordering of a *kosmos* no longer could or should be looked for except beginning with "this world here."

Incarnation and resurrection therefore say nothing other than this: the task of making sense falls to us humans, mortals, who have no gods or nature, who are technicians engaged in the indefinite production of "our" world. But since sense is not "made"—is not produced—it falls to us to recognize how it can take place. It can do so only in the relation that opens at once between us (us, both humans and all beings) and in us, which addresses us simultaneously to one another and—singly and severally—to an opening in us whereby is signaled an infinite referring and a referring to the infinite: yes, we are beings of sense; yes, the world's sense is that we are charged with sense; and yes, the truth of sense is neither completion nor significant plenitude, but rather a suspense whereby sense is at once interrupted and infinitely relaunched.

Incarnation is not the provisional sojourn of god in flesh but the "word made flesh," or flesh itself as sense. It is the body as the visible image of the invisible, the manifestation of what is not manifest. Resurrection is not a second life, but the self-righting movement [*redressement*] whereby the horizontal course of a life turns into a vertical signal. And this is also flesh, for this proper, irreplaceable life thus rights itself. This is also a manifestation of what is not manifest—of sense and of truth. Together incarnation and resurrection interpret a single thought: the body is the event of spirit. Its advent, its coming [venue] to the world, its unexpected arrival [survenue], its irruption, and its passage. This also means: spirit does not hold itself outside the world, it opens in its midst.

Does this create a greeting [salut]? Yes, the mystery that gathers the three mysteries is indeed that of the greeting. But this greeting is neither a saving [sauvetage] nor a salvation [salut]. It is not sheltered outside the world and beyond the reach of death. It takes place right here among us, it is in relation itself. Jacques Derrida was the first to address this "salut without salvation."⁹ "Salut!"—as we say it and hurl it between us in order to salute one another, that is to say, not to save ourselves but to recognize one another as being responsible for sense, or a sense, or, more indistinctly, for senses. "Salut!" as a punctuation of truth: neither prolonging nor, even less, completing sense, at once holding it in suspense and opening its possibility.¹⁰

In such a situation, how are we to understand the "sin" that Christian salvation is supposed to atone for, pardon, redeem? First of all, sin is not defined by fault. It is less a question of the sin than of the sinner. That man should be charged with "original sin" is surely the Judeo-Christian invention that seems most foreign and unacceptable to modern consciousness (one could perhaps point to its Muslim echo: in Islam too, only faith saves). This consciousness persists in understanding sin as fault. But that is not what sin is; it is the condition of mankind closed in on itself.¹¹ When recourse to sacrifice is unavailable and when tragedy no longer permits "joy in mourning" (which is perhaps in some way the sacrifice of oneself), fault—having failed to keep to the divine order(s), the order(s) of the world—becomes the very being of he who cannot absolve himself from it: absolution can come only from the opening of another relation, in another order, which is precisely the order of relation, of sense, of referring within the world to what exceeds the world in itself.

In this sense, sins are pardoned—Nietzsche justly perceived how Christianity was tied together by this certainty, whose somber flip side (the sinning consciousness and the improbable grace of moral Christianity¹²) twisted and even perverted the regime of subjectivity. It is not that no fault can be committed: but it no longer involves disobeying an order that sacrifice or tragic death could redeem. It is—more grave, in a sense, and opening the door to puritanisms—the refusal of relation, of "salut!" Not only is it no longer a matter of disobeying an order, but it gives way to the need to invent a relation where no cosmo-theological order is given.

Pardoning sins goes hand in hand with the possibility of a voluntaristic evil, one sought in the closure of relation and sense, to the profit of an order supposedly fixed, given, and supplied with a completed meaning (with a truth supposedly full, like that of a model for man, for society, and finally for truth). Pardon means that the possibility of sense always remains open: but it does not mean that those who close it, those who condemn this opening, are pardoned. This is perhaps the meaning of the "sin against spirit," which is the only one that will not be pardoned.[13]

Nietzsche again: "Everything breaketh, everything is integrated anew; eternally buildeth itself the same house of being. All things separate, all things again greet one another; eternally true to itself remaineth the ring of being."[14] The sense of "being" [*l'être*] or rather the sense of being [*d'être*] is nothing but sense itself: a separation and a salutation that is addressed, a separation that renders this address (or its refusal) possible.

5

Thus the theologal virtues are the forces that are at work in relation. This is unambiguously signaled by their disposition or declension in three modes—faith, hope, and charity—of which the third, which can also be named love (we shall come to this), is the most important, the one that definitively assures the true stakes of all three, which is to say, the true stakes of the relation to "God."[15]

In order to understand how the commandment to love—the originality, the bizarrerie, the scandal of Christianity—could appear as the keystone of the entire construction, more novel than any other, we must attempt to understand what could have called it forth, and from what region completely different from that of "religion" strictly construed. Christian love did not spring up from the ground as a mushroom (whether edible or poisonous) might. It arrived unexpectedly in a world where a considerable metamorphosis of the cosmic, natural, political, economic, and cultural orders had endangered and perhaps brought to breaking point the possibility of a relation of people to each other and to the world. The order of Rome, however imposing its success might have been, ended up no longer recognizing itself as a possibility of sense. If the fall of the Roman Empire has passed into history and legend as such a considerable and profoundly disquieting phenomenon, that is because it testified to a disruption whose depth and anthropological stakes (or existential or civilizational ones, so to speak) were without precedent in human memory. At the time there was little memory of the fall of the great pre-Greek empires, of an entire succession of upheavals that culture had archived only sparingly—and to which the fulminations of the God of Israel against the empires of Egypt and Babylon bore witness, in a semi-mythological way. But the fall of Rome undoubtedly appeared, visibly and expressly, as, for the first time, the end of a whole world.

This world had been, in a manner constant since the most ancient times, across empires and across agrarian and civil religions, a world of observance—that is to say, of what defines, in the most proper way, *religio*, the scrupulous observance (of rules, of rituals) of which Rome provided, in that word, the most precise image (to the point of mania . . .). What had been coming to the surface since the slow pre-Greek and pre-Jewish evolutions and revolutions, if one can put it this way, was what I shall risk characterizing by a single trait: the substitution of a world of relation for the world of observance. Of course, relation does not simply exclude observance: but it subordinates it. What with alphabetic writing, coinage, commercial and especially maritime practices (journeys, trading posts), then with cities, the techniques of *logos* and of law, and mathematics practiced for itself, the regime of observance was being overwhelmed on all sides. It was also being overwhelmed insofar as it properly comprised domination by the principles of observance and their representatives. A hierarchical world, in the full sense of the term, was being called into question. What the Greeks named "philosophy" attempted to respond to this state of affairs, while, in a completely different vein, the exodus from Egypt invented trust in a covenant set apart from such domination: all of which is to say that our history was beginning, the one that we are attempting to grasp in order to understand better what it wants from us.

☞

(We know that twenty centuries of history did not proceed in a linear fashion. They passed through many variations in the sharing [*partage*], contrast, and antinomy of what I have gathered under the words *observance* and *relation*. But this history began with the mutation that I am attempting to characterize, and the "flight of the gods," then the monotheisms, and especially Christianity, have been its echo chamber. Between the Renaissance and the nineteenth century, this history believed that it could understand itself as "rationality" and thus account for its history as the progress of humanity. But we are now discovering that this reason still needs to dis-enclose itself in order to welcome everything that was not "progress"—nor regression either—but that was thrusting the mutation forward out of the most archaic or neglected depths of the "human" phenomenon and, by way of it, of the event called "world." Here we are only at the beginning—at least if dis-enclosure is not, to the contrary, the end of the same event. But the very fact that we must now think a destruction of mankind and of the world testifies to the amplitude of the mutation.)

ॐ

Two phenomena, which the Christian invention echoes, stand out in the general transformation of the Mediterranean world, where the unheard-of possibility of thinking a "world" in its totality was being sketched out (something of "globalization" was latent in Rome). They are the phenomena of violence and riches set apart from regimes of observance. Relations of force and property relations are present and active everywhere: but when the cultures of observance and hierarchy break down, these two registers of relation ("social," if you will, but also profoundly human, existential) are emancipated, so to speak, and take on characteristics that distinguish them from their previous states.

Why are violence and riches—non-violence and poverty—salient motifs in Christianity, just as they had started to be in philosophy?[16] Why is the evangelists' condemnation of riches so pitiless? Why does Jesus chase the merchants out of the Temple? Why does he speak of "turning the other cheek"? The later involvement of the Christian religions with power and money is of little consequence, for with it they entered into a grave self-contradiction and were constrained to hear themselves accused, always anew, by their faithful, even if the churches themselves didn't want to know about it. The important thing to understand is that, in the mutation we are discussing, power and money—and the two as buttressing one another—took off in an autonomous deployment, one of whose later names would be "capitalism" (Marx calls Antiquity "pre-capitalism"), and another "imperialism" (which essentially refers to a mode of domination different from that of the Empires of long ago).

In this way appears a naked poverty, a poverty of injustice and exclusion that nothing justifies—where, previously, appeared an exaltation of riches (monuments, treasure, the pomp of courts and temples from Memphis or Susa to Athens and Jerusalem) that did not signify, or not simply, the despoilment of someone else.[17] In the same way, a naked, unarmed weakness appears, exposed to blows but claiming another kind of confident force. Nietzsche is not wrong to discern a thrusting forward of the weak in the Judeo-Christian mind, but he does not perceive clearly enough the transformation force undergoes when weakness is proclaimed in a way that cannot be reduced to resentment: in the absence of a legitimation, if not a transfiguration into divine glory—that would require the whole apparatus of an observance—force and riches captured and accumulated for themselves gravely wound the relation in whose bosom they are deployed.

This is the daunting ambiguity of the mutation: the relation that it promotes is also what it threatens. Where observance and belonging provided linkages (even if we judge these bonds to be painful, their most gripping form for us being slavery), the blossoming of relation breaks down links in two antithetical ways: it detaches itself from observance and belonging, and it also distends the relation that it must form.[18] Capitalized force and riches, if we can use the expression, lead to the call of weakness and injustice for a different justice. We know only too well that we have not finished with the expansion of this movement, and we also know how much "human rights" and "socialisms" are the inheritors of Christianity. But with "right" [droit] and "society," we find ourselves back within reason's enclosure.

6

Charity attempts to respond otherwise than through law and society. It has quite rightly been judged vile because of the hypocrisy that can hide beneath it to escape the demands of justice. Can one imagine how its power, its impulsion, might be given (back) to it?

Meditating on human violence as he saw it unleashed in the First World War—the beginning, perhaps, of what is perhaps the last phase of the mutation—Freud declares that he can name only one response equal to these stakes: the Christian commandment to love.[19] Of course, he judges it to be impracticable, sees in it the exorbitant demand of the "Superego of civilization," and finds nothing there capable of dampening his pessimism in the face of the gravity of civilization's malady, or that civilization itself is—a malady that, precisely, is not a "malady," does not lend itself to a therapeutic schema, but well and truly represents "evil" [mal] and "unhappiness" [malheur]. But he nonetheless underlines the unique character of love's response, as if, on the one hand, he had a premonition that the possibility of modern violence was already given in the epoch that produced Christianity, and, on the other, he could recognize in this impracticable "love" at least the justness of a sign, a signal, even if not that of an instrument.

What does the word caritas say? It states the fact of attaching a price, of treating something as dear [cher] (carus). This Latin transcription of Greek agapē keeps the latter's quality of a favorable welcome, of a considerateness or elective benevolence even as it inscribes itself in the lexicon of prices and value.[20] Contrary to riches as an end in themselves, charity affirms a unique, exclusive, and incommensurable price, which must be the price of everyone. (What else have we been affirming in speaking since Kant of human "dignity"? But as soon as it was enunciated, this evaporated into abstraction).

Perhaps all this is indeed impracticable, certainly so if we mix up with it the values of tenderness and desire also understood to be part of "love." But perhaps here the impossible is the very index of truth: that relation—and I shall risk adding the relation with all beings—has no sense unless each one of its terms ("subjects") can be allocated an exclusive, singular value. That only desire and tenderness, only *eros* innervating *agapē* can manifest this exclusivity, and only in an exclusive manner, between specific beings, is one thing, but there is no doubt that this exclusivity is due to all. Lovers are outside the world: but whether it shows or not, they are charged with this "outside" on behalf of everyone. Without that, we would have to renounce conceiving of mankind and the world, we would have to give everything over again to observances—for example, to castes, to the juxtaposed states dignity and indignity, and so on.

If love declares the impossible itself ("madness," says Christianity), if it puts forward a gesture as exorbitant for the one who receives it as for the one who gives—if this distinction is even possible—and if it definitively escapes the mastery that would, strictly speaking, allow "giving" and "receiving," this "madness," which extends from erotic fury to spiritual fervor, consists entirely in this: in it relation becomes incandescent by addressing me to what, in the other, is incommensurable with me, and it also does so by starting out with what is incommensurable in me. Thus love attests that everyone is unique, but with a unicity that exceeds the "one" of everyone. This attestation is properly impossible, it cannot be presented or realized, but it is what naked existence calls for, existence without a world-beyond and without essence.[21]

If one does not give up on conceiving of mankind and the world, without reducing them to the observances that civilization has taken apart—at the cost of its "malaise," but also gaining in the same movement a sense of the exclusive worth of each existence—then we must understand that the civilization that for a time called itself "Christian" called for a commandment of universal love in response to a demand come from further away than a religion, come from a mutation in civilization itself. On this view, "love" is neither a penchant nor an affection, even if it can create space for penchants, affections, and passions: love is first of all a way of thinking. It is of the order of those "thoughts that do not return to the self—pure élans" that Levinas discusses and that think through the experience of the other [*autrui*].[22] There is not even any need to invoke the ethical visage of *autrui*: it is enough to feel the power of the "outside" that is borne by, or bears, *autrui*. Love is always, even in erotic love, a way of thinking in the sense of the experience of something real, if "real" always means "outside": this is what it is, it must be "outside" for us, above all in the sense of the experience of this real, which is the relation among all existents that, strictly speaking, *makes* the world, as soon as this world lacks any other world. This is what renders this experience everyone's due.

This is why the love called "Christian" is strictly indissociable from equality. Kierkegaard puts it rigorously: "since the neighbour is every human being, unconditionally every human being, all dissimilarities are indeed removed from the object, and therefore this love is recognizable precisely by this, that its object is without any of the more precise specifications of dissimilarity, which means that this love is recognizable only by love."[23] This love is therefore due to everyone, not via a tender sentiment extended toward each and every one, by turns or en masse, but because in itself it is essentially and, in effect, uniquely the position of equality.

Due to everyone, but not only "by right" [*en droit*]. As soon as one stands within the law or limits oneself to law—whose necessity is not in any doubt, of course—one risks losing a certain power. I do not mean the power to appeal to a charitable impulse or generosity. It does not involve sentiments but making sense. It thus always concerns feeling [*sentir*], but feeling insofar as we enter into relation only by also relating to the incommensurable that is designated by the "dignity," the "worth," and the singular "value" of each existence. Only at this price, this priceless price, will we be able to honor the stakes of relation: the stakes of being in the world shared among men and among all beings.

Adoration is addressed to this worth, to this inestimable value: it is the evaluation of what cannot be evaluated. Because we are swept up there, thrust there, this is why we must understand virtue as the energy of the drive. Why this thrust? Because mankind is the being of sense and because sense—which we can also name value—cannot be evaluated. It is absolute value. The "love of others," in its apparently sentimental silliness and in its impossibility as a real disposition—for psychology as much as for sociology—simply indicates the value toward which we are turned by the simple fact of our fortuitous existence, whether we wish so or not, whether we believe in it or not, insofar as we are taken up in sense or as our being is a being of sense. This value is absolute because it has the plurality of all existences themselves. It is the "value" in itself of the echoing, the referring of all existences among themselves. The being of the world is a being of sense—and it is so either in itself or through us, which comes down to the same thing, since we are ourselves of the world, but we are what in the world opens as its outside—an outside that, alone, gives the world its true "worldly" dimension: the possibility, the power, and the dynamics of relation.

7

The drive to sense—to sense and to the truth that is suspended in it—is in us and through us the only thing that can, beyond justice, or rather, as the very excellence (the hyperbolic value) of justice, displace the regime of power and money as we know it. Which is to say: it is the only thing that can displace what we designate by capital and technology, or what designates itself more and more visibly as the indefinite accumulation of ends in the generalized devastation of dignity. In still other words: it drifts beyond the "malaise" if not beyond the disaster of civilization.

What do the two other virtues attempt to do? They are simply at the service of the third. Faith is given as nothing other than the force of trust in that (or him, or her, or those) of which it is impossible for me to obtain any knowledge that would create any assurance or guarantee.[24] Unlike belief, a weak knowledge that nonetheless arms itself with various guarantees, plausibilities, or non-impossibilities, faith exposes itself to non-knowledge: not to ignorance, but to the excess beyond knowledge. But without faith, we could not enter into the sphere of sense, which is to say, above all into that of language. To accede to speech is to have already been thrust forward by a trust in sense and in the fact that the other invites me to sense. Children do not learn languages by instinct or by mimicry: they learn because others have opened the space of this trust to them. This is what allowed Derrida to speak of "that which in faith acquiesces before or beyond all questioning, in the already common experience of a language and of a 'we.'"[25] For this reason, faith in "God" in the sense of all monotheism is a trust in a god that is unknown, unknowable, unappropriable in any form: neither master, nor king, nor judge, nor, finally, god.

Faith is perhaps best expressed in the following dialogue, where its sense is borne by the verb *to believe*:

> TEMPLE: . . . Is there a heaven, Nancy?
> NANCY: I don't know. I believes.
> TEMPLE: Believe what?
> NANCY: I don't know. But I believes.[26]

As for hope [*espérance*], it most properly designates the tension internal to the drive: not the hope [*espoir*] that something—an answer, a conclusion—might come about, but the tension retained in the trust that something or someone always *comes*. And that it will come not later but here and now—not coming in order to complete itself in a presence, but so that I come thanks to its coming. No analogy is more fitting here than that of sexual joy and *jouissance*: not satisfaction, not the easing of tension, not becoming replete, but the infinite relational tension between two bodies, which is to say, between two drives caught up in their contact, which is both sensitive and beyond sense.

Drive, a thrust coming from elsewhere, from outside, from nowhere, which opens up in us; which comes from there but which, at the same time, opens up this unlocalizable place; which comes from mystery and produces it, which triggers its flash and goes back into its night: to the absence of solution, to the dis-solution where truth resides. But in this truth is kept and saluted the existence of everyone; the impulsion of relation and the pulsation of sense: it comes and goes from one to the other, from some to others, without establishing any continuity of being but rhythming our common presence—our co-appearance [*comparution*] and our exposure [*exposition*].

Definitively, the drive is us. It is the movement, the coming, the unexpected arrival, the life, the existence that we are. Its beating, its breathing, are the displacement, plasticity, and mutation that we are. It is our inequality, our heterogeneity to "ourselves," the tension and thrust coming from the force that separates the world from elsewhere, separates something from nothing: a drive of being, being as a drive in whose charge we find ourselves, an infinite gap from any being posed in itself. Sense, language, sentiment of existing.

༜

Truth: not a being [*être*], nor of a being [*être*], but true existence. Without signification but endowed with the sense of being saluted. To conclude, it is a name. Just as "God" is or was a name, the unnamable name of the Jewish and Muslim gods, a common noun [*nom*], which took on the capital letter of a proper noun with the Christian God, but which also took the name of a man. It thus became all names, became the unpronounceable part of all names, what remains unnamable in each "proper" noun because it does not signify—and perhaps not only men but also all beings have a name?

Drive: an attraction, a desire, a pleasure. Simply to relate to one another, simply to name one another and to glimpse one another in passing in this world, and this world itself passing between nothing and nothing. "Each perceiving being feels joy in perceiving what it perceives."[27] In the impetus that pushes it toward this joy, there is more than a force that simply thrusts: this force goes beyond itself; in other words, "drive" names what in a general force inscribes it within a difference from itself. Not only does a difference between forces belong to force in itself, but the thrust of force is what carries it beyond itself. A drive goes toward something other than itself, which is not to say that it has an "object" in the normal sense of the term: it goes toward what cannot feature as an object. One could say: it is a subject that goes toward greater being or greater sense, toward the increase [*surcroît*] that it truly "is" itself. Insofar as it regards the world, for example, it feels itself regarded by it; insofar as it speaks, as it feels itself thrust in and by language beyond language—and beyond silence too.

Adoration: the movement and the joy of recognizing ourselves as existents in the world. Not that this existence is not tough, thankless, shot through with grief. Yet this grief is not the price we pay in order to reach another world. It redeems nothing, but at least we can, insofar as we do not give up on living, salute and name some beings from time to time. To adore passes through naming, saluting the unnamable that the name hides within it and that is nothing other than the fortuitousness of the world.

8

If the destruction of an illusion only creates a little more ignorance, as the epigraph to this chapter has it, then once the illusion of God is destroyed, the ignorance created is the ignorance of all that there could be in God's place. And yet adoration causes us to receive this ignorance as truth: not a *docta ignorantia*, perhaps not even a "non-knowledge," nothing that would still attempt to regain assurance in the negative, but the simple, naked truth that there is nothing in the place of God because there is no place for God. The outside of the world opens us in the midst of the world, and there is no first or final place. Each one of us is at once the first and the last. Each one, each name. And our ignorance is aggravated by the fact that we do not know whether or not we ought to name this common and singular property of all names—for instance, by naming it "God" once again (another, a totally other god? . . .). Or indeed by giving it all our names. Or indeed by risking the word *unnamable*, which not by chance with Beckett has become a master-word—even a master-name— but which is always creating the conditions necessary to project us either toward a vile sort of discharge or toward an ineffable beyond that would reproduce lost illusions. It is in this suspense that we must hold ourselves for the moment, hesitating and stammering between various possible languages, in sum, learning to speak anew.

ॐ

Nietzsche writes: "Supposing that faith in God has disappeared, the question is asked anew: 'Who is speaking?'" He continues: "My response is taken not from metaphysics but from animal physiology: the herd instinct is speaking."[28]

Doubtless Nietzsche was not wrong, because we have not known how to make anything speak other than democracy, law, and the automaton's addition of one technique to another. Henceforth it falls to us to be capable of another response. Not the herd, but *us*—an unsituateable subject that appears each time in an *I*, but an *I* that can, that knows how to—whatever the nature of this knowledge may be—speak for *us* (which is to say, at once "in our name" and "addressing us"). And the speech in question must be addressed—only being able to be addressed to *us* if it is above all outside—to the immensity of the outside that opens up in the very midst of our world and that therefore tells us something about the senseless sense of this world.

This response would not be opposed to Nietzsche's. But it would attempt to overcome what was an obstacle for him: the representation of democracy as a general regime of equalization, not of men but of "values," which is to say, a regime of a leveling of sense. This requires above all that we understand that "democracy" carries with it more than a political form, that it is more than the assumption of all the spheres of existence into politics. I shall not dwell here on what I have sketched out elsewhere.[29] All that matters is to affirm that adoration, the addressing of speech to what lies outside any possible speech, is a condition of "democratic" existence understood as the existence of equal subjects. For the equality of "subjects"—to give them this name in the absence of any better one—is not that of individuals. The equality of individuals can concern a juridical equivalence and an economic equity, but from the outset it is exposed not to inequality but to the intrinsic heterogeneity of all singular relations to the incommensurable. For the latter, one could never propose any rule of equalization or unequalization.

ॐ

The adorent [*adorant*] is not a worshipper [*adorateur*]: he does not commit to venerating an idol. In the idol, one imagines that one recognizes, feels, and respects a power (from which one can expect some sort of protective, charitable, or salutary effect). The adorent holds himself within an address that comes to him from somewhere other than an imposition of power and that goes somewhere other than toward homage to the powerful and the quest for favors. His address is already a response, and it responds neither to order nor to authority. It is speech that somehow responds only to itself: to its own opening, to the possibility given within language of going to the limit of significations and as far as silence—and even further than silence, as far as song, as music. Which is to say, it goes toward what holds the present open, infinitely open to a coming that no present or presence can contain and that for this reason is constantly returning. Music: the eternal return of the beginning and the end, of one in the other, the return of the *eternal* as such, which is to say, as what opens and suspends time. I repeat that Augustine says to sing is to pray twice: the second time raises prayer beyond any demand or expectation.

Indeed, it is adoration that carries and holds the adorent, and not the other way around. It does not lay down a respect or an allegiance—it may well involve respect and allegiance, but not in the first instance: for above all, adoration lies within an impetus that does not measure anything in a hierarchical way. It can even be said to be anarchic and to get carried away, lifted up by something lying well beyond any measure, any distribution of roles. It is nothing other, at least in the form in which it is born, than the movement of singing that comes to the throat and the lips for no reason, from nowhere, in an uncertain cadence, in a tune still lacking precise melody, and in an issuing that is withdrawn from the formed, speaking voice.

This song would be held and stretched between the full, worked-out form of the *oratorio* and the formlessness of *humming* [*fredonnement*]— whose name takes us back to babbling or spluttering and even to the chirping of birds and the thrumming of cicadas. The murmur and stammering of a celebration and an invocation, of an exclamation that comes from before language and outlasts it. A salutation without salvation, which salutes existence, a stranger to the opposition between the saved and the lost, the blessed and the damned. Or again: the world saluting itself, via all of "nature" up to "mankind" and its "technology," engendered by nature in order to get to the end of its creation [*art*]: a know-how of the impossible, the incommensurable, and the infinite—the revelation that the world is not there in order to remain there, laid down on itself, but on the contrary in order to open this "there" onto unheard-of, exalting or catastrophic, sublime or monstrous distancings, and perhaps all of this comes down to a single coming. A sole, unique, trembling coming, perilous and yet resolved, which is also the coming of song itself, its beating.

4

Complements, Supplements, Fragments

When we are stirred to lament the loss of the gods, it is more than likely the gods who are doing the stirring.[1]

Beatitude

A fixed syntagm makes it easy to speak of "beatific adoration," meaning bleating devotion, irresponsible submission, even insidiously masochistic allegiance. The fixed nature of this expression indicates that one can understand the noun after the adjective as simply redundant: adoration would be in essence "beatific." And it would be contentedly imbecilic in its blind submission. But we do not know how things stand with beatitude here, nor with submission.

Beatitude, the state of "blessedness" [*bienheureux*] that is the sense of the word, is subject to the law stating that certain terms which should be understood as actions are understood as states: pleasure, charm, felicity, joy, *jouissance* (even happiness can perhaps be listed here). We tend too readily to consider the series of notions or representations that could be grouped together under the generic term "agreeable" as accomplished states rather than as things in the process of unfolding. (By contrast, what is "disagreeable" does not allow us to forget that the act continues to act: the torments of pain, difficulty, and unhappiness are unending.)

Here it's like the logics of "*jouissance*" and "fulfillment," which I shall discuss later: what fulfills itself [*se comble*] does not limit itself to completion [*complétion*], but overflows fulfillment [*complétude*] itself. Strictly speaking, beatitude cannot consist in being "beatific" [*béat*], given that homophony brings it close to a gaping [*béant*]: a contented, foolish sprawling (whether pious, voluptuous, or gluttonous, as you will). The truth of pleasure is in desire.[2] The truth of beatitude is in a movement that responds to a call, and this response differs in nature from a response to a question. Indeed, the latter can satisfy or resolve the question, whereas the former launches the call still further, maintains it for longer.

As we know, Spinoza wrote in the last proposition of his *Ethics*: "Blessedness is not the reward of virtue, but is virtue itself." In demonstrating this proposition, he specifies that "blessedness consists in love towards God . . . [and] must be related to mind in so far as it acts."[3] In the same way, adoration is not (and has no) realization in any completion whatsoever. It consists entirely in tension, drive, impetus. Of course, it is familiar with rhythms, even the arhythmia of a heartbeat, but not with "beatific" appeasement.

On the contrary, evil can consist in such a completion—satisfaction, assuagement, contentedness, solution. Here one turns away from the infinite, one becomes complacent in immobility. This is what it means to condemn "idols." An idol is an idol when its worshipper [*adorateur*] is satisfied with worshipping it [*l'adorer*]: any God or devil can become an idol in this way and perhaps always has the tendency to do so.

Yet the submission, veneration, and prostration toward which adoration can turn do not necessarily bear the sign of humiliation, renunciation of dignity. On the contrary, they can proceed from the noblest and proudest act. This is how, for example, the entire sense of Islam—of "trusting submission," as we said above—is played out around the interpretation of this submission. That God's will should be "you shall worship only Him," can be understood as setting aside any allegiance to any powers or idols whatsoever, including God himself if worshipped as an idol.[4]

Excessive Speech

"Beyond silence": it seemed possible to characterize adoration thus. But beyond silence lies no more profound or more silent silence. Instead, one must return to language. Silence is always more or less considered as a hyperbolic language, as a reserve of sense exceeding words and rich with its own secret, its own intimacy. In this sense, one speaks sometimes of "mute adoration," being dumbstruck figuring the withheld, hesitant obverse of that to which silence gives an eloquent face. To return to a language beyond silence means cutting to the quick of language, to what within it neither declares nor names in a strict sense, without wilting at the approach of an Unnamable.

To the quick: where language speaks only in a paradoxical trust in its own uncertainty, in its own inadequacy, as we are accustomed to say. This trust—which is truly the very *reason* of language in all senses of the word *reason*—seems to go beyond any assurance in signification or in an ultimate Sense beyond all signs.

But language constantly makes significations shift, play, tremble. This is how it speaks, and this is how it knows it is a language: it subsists in approximation, in what shifts. Where does it come from? From the non-place that opens in the midst of the world and beginning with which things open, shift, and happen, things constantly replay this coming, this approach, and this shifting, this trembling in which everything comes about: the world, life, sense, the thing, all of them fortuitous, uncertain, vibrating, unsteady.

Thus speech is addressed to what sovereignly exceeds it; its worth as speech is as access to this excess, an access that opens through "mankind" onto the totality of the world's existents and to the outside that divides and shares [*partage*] them, that they divide and share among themselves; man, the one who speaks, exists in the name of, on behalf of, we could even say as a consequence of [*en raison de*] the totality of the world's existents: he receives his reason for being as the one who must give accounts of or reasons for [*rendre raison de*] the world. He gives reasons for what is without reason—the fortuitous, the die as cast, our lot as shared: a reason that is not unreasonable, but perhaps without reason. Excessive speech is dedicated to this. Its proffering must indefinitely be taken up anew, remodulated, relaunched, repeated in interminable variations, because its theme—what is without reason, reason without reason—never appears outside of these variations or their profusion. Ibn Arabi writes: "All beings present in the world stand together equally in God, due to the store of trust that mankind possesses."[5] This store of trust is speech, it is the opening of sense—an opening that is not followed by any closure.

Excessive speech speaks indefinitely, in the exuberance of literary inventions, the profusion of fictions, and the proliferation of discourses, but it also speaks infinitely—and then one no longer hears it, there is nothing more to hear. It resonates only in the voice itself, in a murmur, a rubbing of the voice against itself, hesitating on the threshold of speech. This is the extreme intimacy of the voice, the buried heart of language, a groaning of suffering or of *jouissance*, a brushing up against sense. The two modes of speaking are created back to back with one another, and by one another: orality both oratory and adoring.

This means it is the gods who make us speak. Language is divine insofar as it comes from the outside and returns toward it (also turning itself around), toward this outside that it itself opens in us, by opening our mouths, and by opening this strange sign, "man," in the midst of the world. But this also means that the "gods" are themselves language through and through: they are names, myths, calls. Monotheism (and with it, but quite differently, Buddhism) has represented god essentially, even exclusively, as something that speaks. God is therefore effaced in speech, confused with call and response, and thus becomes the unnamable.

But this means yet more. The unnamable is a function of language: there is only nomination against a backdrop of the unnamable, and the latter is nothing other than what is said in all nomination. One could say: the unnamable is not ineffable. Naming opens toward the unreachable, to the irreducibility of the thing, the real, the existent. Only language gives this opening, but it is also alone in designating this opening as a gaping toward the infinite, outside language and yet always repeated anew, demanded again in speech.

In this sense we must also understand that adoration creates its own "object." No particular thing or being is given in the infinite distancing of everything that is given and to which we could relate at the limit of language. But there are speaking beings who make it evident that their speech speaks beyond itself; it does not speak about a beyond, it speaks beyond. Thus it does nothing other than create the world: it relates existences to the *nothing* that is the ground from which they detach themselves and relate to one another. The universe in its expansion, the profusion of beings, living beings impelled by their desire, the beating of all the signals that are exchanged, all of this is taken up by and is at play in the speaking drive that also makes it appear—because this drive names the universe, the living being, the sign—while also making it retreat further into the infinity of sense.

It is by speaking beyond itself and beyond sense that speech opens sense. In fact, speech receives itself from the beyond even before it speaks: it is what, in the speaking animal, has already animated it in order for it to speak. In the vocal cords, the tongue, the entire phonatory apparatus, as in the neuronal reticulations where symbolization is activated, "nature" has already addressed speech. Without finality: as the excess in it of the proper sense of speech, of the proper fact of its existence. A mystic expressed it thus: "I thought I was invoking Him, yet His invocation preceded my own; I thought I was soliciting Him and knew Him, but His knowledge preceded mine; I felt that I loved Him, and yet He loved me first, and I imagined that I adored him, whereas He had already put the creatures of the earth at my service."[6] "He" is unnamable, and the "service" that "creatures" perform is neither service to he who speaks here nor to mankind—but service to adoration itself, which, passing through "me," infinitely returns from speech to speech.

"It is quite possible that life's splendor resides beside each being and always in its fullness, but that it is veiled, hidden in the depths, invisible . . ., yet that if it is invoked by the right word, by its true name, it will come forth."[7]

Adoration and Reduction

Adoration is contrasted, above all, to reduction. I do not exempt here the "phenomenological reduction," the suspension of the supposedly spontaneous and unreflecting attitude that allegedly prevents us from discerning what truly makes up our relation to the world and to ourselves. I am neither contesting nor criticizing this: I am deliberately starting from a different point, not face-to-face with the world, myself, or *autrui*, but in a *being-in-the-world* that, just like Heidegger's *in der Welt sein*, which I have translated in this way in order to render its intention (which the German itself renders badly), is not a "being placed within" something that would contain it, but a belonging, or better, an inherence, or still better, a mutual intrication or enveloping, such that "I" am not "in" the world, but rather that *I am the world* and the world is me, just as it is you and us, the wolf and the lamb, nitrogen, iron, optical fibers, black holes, lichen, fantastical imagery, thought, and the thrust of "things" themselves. These things that are and make up the world are nothing other than the relations among all existents—these relations that we constantly diversify, complicate, multiply, modify, model, and modulate in the indefinite resumption of a song without melody, words, or even the timbre of a voice and that nonetheless we constantly—even as we lose it, suppress it, and find it anew—address to this: that there is the world, that it is given, given as abandoned, this singular admixture of being and non-being, of finite and infinite, of life and death, of sense and the senseless that is named "existence."

The world of existence or existences is precisely the ensemble of relations that never make up "a" world, even less a world of objects facing subjects, but—if we are to stay with this terminology—a world that is itself "subject": subject of the relations of which it is the general connectedness. A subject of relations means definitively a subject that in itself— like all subjects—is relation and nothing but relation: a being-to, to itself/to the same/to nothing, a being whose entire being consists in the *to*. Ultimately, the *Destruktion* of ontology that Heidegger desired can be transcribed in this way: there is no "being"; *being* designates an act or rather an indefinite complex of acts made up by the relations without which the very terms (or subjects) of these relations would not exist. A relation: an address, call, invitation, refusal, rejection, signal, desire, even an indifference, or an avoiding taking place through the abundance of existences. Which *exist* by dint of thus *exposing* themselves according to relation.

Thus, no difference between "being" [*l'être*] and "being" [*l'étant*] but this *différance* that Derrida named—or unnamed—which signals that the existent exposes itself and does only that: creates a gap from itself, not a distance that could defer its final advent, but rather a proximity whose open chink puts it into contact with the totality of beings and thus with the infinite of the opening that shares them all and reunites them all. It reunites them to nothing other than this opening itself: to the open of the world, to the open that is the world and about which all we can say is that we must attempt to adore it. That is, to address to it the witness of existence itself. Finally, what I am naming "to adore" here means: deciding to exist, deciding on existence, turning aside from non-existence, from the closure of the world on itself. (A world closed on itself is a Sense gained, an ultimate Goal [*Fin*], a world reduced to a something, to something far less than a pebble).

෴

Our culture has dedicated itself to another reduction, seen in the maxim "Myths are fables," that is, they are illusory and untruthful inventions. One called this "the thinking of suspicion"—namely, suspicion of any form of the absolute, the ideal, the unconditional. These three words themselves inevitably provoke suspicion. And yet *they are necessary!* By this I mean that we should be able to not reduce them.

There is little point in getting bogged down by demonstrating that we must not return to myth. The idea of a "new mythology" refuses to cease smoldering—and indeed sometimes rises up in terrifying flames. But we must avoid reducing what could be called a mythical but not mythifying function, and which would take up or put into play anew or otherwise the role that myths played in their cultures: not to give explanations relying on a state of knowledge different from our own, which would therefore be wrong and illusory for us, but expressing an experience (e.g., the presence of the dead, the fascinating power of fire, the begetting of children, etc.) that is ultimately an experience of unlimitedness, of incommensurability, of an extravagance experienced as being inscribed within nature, life, the exorbitant order of the world.

This is the sense in which Freud wrote "drives are our myths": forces that thrust us from far before ourselves to far beyond ourselves—as far as life/death, intimacy/strangeness, absorbing/rejecting the outside. These forces cause us to experience, we are even the experience of them, without it being possible for us to assign them the status of physical or physiological forces, without our being able to identify them as instincts or intentions, without our being able to identify *ourselves* as tropistic organisms or as subjects gifted with consciousness. But in us, through us, and as us the power of what does not allow itself to be reduced to these identities (organism, consciousness) is in play: a relation to "self" as to an infinite outside.

"Our myths" also means: for us who no longer have myths. Drives are the mythology of a mankind without myths. A pure mythology in some way: without the figures of gods or of heroes, without marvelous events, being only the unfigurable thrust of what attempts to live by producing sense, relation, the world, and discovers that it is also a death drive, a drive to destroy beings and relationships. According to Freud, drives are essentially plastic: they can displace, transform, and lead astray their objects, and this is why we can speak of "drives," the plurality of a unique, obscure, indefinite thrust.

But this thrust is nothing other than the repetition of the originary beating within us, of the opening of the world, only an "origin" in this beating which is always anterior and posterior to itself, retraction of necessity/expansion of fortuitousness, a throwing of existents into the world—birth and abandonment conjoined. Nothing other than this beating drives us, nothing else drives within us, through us. This is what is repeated as language: the beating of sense and its suspense, of its address and dissemination.

Incarnation/Struction

Universality and incarnation: no other civilization in the history of humanity has represented its own essence or destiny as the incarnation of the divine (*history* and *humanity* being themselves creations of this civilization, its products and its driving principles)—but incarnation also opens up an infinite pity, because it carries within it an ontological decline. This is not a decline in contrast to another status, but a "fall" as "being": being as fall, which is to say, as a movement of what lacks a basis, a standpoint, ground. The West is without ground, it is the invention of the absence of grounds *as an initial given*, not even as an "absence" or privation, but the proposition of an *outside* as truth: not a truth "of the inside," but a *true exposition of the inside*, ex-acting or ex-traction as the entire movement in principle.

At the same time, and if the whole of "creation" is indeed at stake in the economy said to pertain to "salvation" [*salut*] (some theologians have argued that the "mystical body of Christ" would incorporate all of nature), we must affirm that I touch the world in its entirety, in the totality of its force and its expansion. This touching engages neither interiority nor exteriority; it allows me neither to possess the world nor to lose myself within it; it establishes between "me" and "the world" a coincidence that is essentially that of the initial opening, of the ex nihilo, of its surprised start [*sursaut*] and jolt [*soubresaut*]. I come into the world with the world itself, and, in the history of nature, man is he who takes up and puts back into play all appearing. This is language. This is also technology, second nature, the supplementing—and then the supplanting—of nature. The indefinite multiplication of beginnings and ends: new eras constantly come to pass, whether with vaccines, steam, electricity, atomic energy—fission and perhaps one day fusion—cybernetics, and new ends are constantly dispersing and dissolving the very idea of an end to nature or to mankind. We are leaving the order of ends entirely behind us, if not that of the unending ends that are the accumulations of production, of "goods," of means (to what ends?), of powers (of transmission, analysis, recombination), of longevity, of the observation of galaxies or of space travel, and at the same time of population, of hunger, of poverty, and of ever more visible tears in the surface of what makes our world a fabric drawn tighter and tighter: to the point where we suspect that we could, in fact, rip everything apart. That we are in a sort of general laceration, as if the regime of relation and of bonds could lead only to rupture, dispersion, and dislocation.

It is as if mankind were recreating in place of the world an ensemble at once more organic—interdependent, interlinked—and more and more accumulative (piled up, juxtaposed, heaped). A *struction*—that is to say, a piling up—without true construction, yet without total destruction. The motif of deconstruction does nothing but update this state of "struction." With it, the contiguity between beings changes its meaning or becomes problematic: it is suspended between the passing by of a sense and the obstruction caused by a jumble. Something like a chaos that would both precede and follow the formation of "elements," "kingdoms," and "species." That would both precede and follow the construction of nature and the instruction of humanity.

The import of the "with" is at stake here: Who desires the diversity of beings, languages, cultures, epochs, persons? It is not enough to have done with gathering them into a transcendental unity. We must know what to do with relation. We must know how to unfold and articulate the demand that Heidegger poses when, elliptically, he says that the "with" of "being with" (*Mitsein*) should not be understood as categorial but as existential (which is to say, not as a simple category of disposition, addition, or juxta-position, but as an intrinsic condition of ek-sistence).

This understanding of the "with"—which Heidegger himself was able to grasp only in the dimension of a "people" and its "destiny," even as "communism" simply made nothing of it, or rather, only the too-well-named "masses"—is very precisely that in relation to which the great, profound, unconscious decisions of relational civilization are played out: exchanges regulated via general equivalence, juridico-political equality, and individual liberty considered as ends in themselves, the vicious circle of ends becoming the means of other ends, which in their turn are means . . .

What I name adoration would be only the consideration of what in relation—relation among us, to oneself, to the world—opens to the infinite, without which there would be no *relation* in the full sense that this word alone, perhaps, can take on, but only rapport, liaison, connection. These and other terms presuppose subjects or entities between which is made a bond that is, in consequence, posterior and subordinated to being. Relation wins out over being, indeed it opens the sense of being, without offending "subjects" in any way: for it does not intervene between those that are already given; it makes them possible, creates them. Is not each one of us engendered by a relation, and should not the world be conceived of as a creation of relations rather than beings [*êtres*]? The difference be-tween night and day, the difference between matters, forms, thoughts . . . The infinite difference of each re-absorption of these differences into a being uniformly reduced to itself.

Incarnation: that divine infinity should be at work in the relation among finite beings. That sense should be in essence finite: interrupted, suspended over empty truth in order to avoid the smothering completion of a conclusion.

Nothing

Our suffering: we know that we are bereft of horizons and, with them, justifications for misfortune (maladies, injustices) and grounds for the punishment of crimes (for the designation of "those who are bad"). This is what is meant by the self-dissolution of the West in the deployment of its in-finite (i.e., lacking ends) logic, which forms the flip side of the logical infinite (where the end in itself is present at each moment: quite distinct from suicide, which affirms a given present as cessation, not as punctuation).

Against this suffering of the in-finite (capital, equivalence, the bad infinite), a differentiation, a different evaluation (Nietzsche), and thus an "adoration" are needed.

Evil, this evil that we now know belongs to our own capacity to turn against one another because we will not turn away toward the infinite, always and in all its forms consists in a closed identification, an idolatry, a figuration without remainder: as soon as I put forward this or that, put forward that this or that "are" the good or the truth of mankind or of the world, I enter into evil. But "relativizing" does not get us out of this situation, for the "relative" can be thought only against the backdrop of the "absolute." The absolute must be affirmed without its relative counterpart, the absolute of each "one," of each "here and now," of each instant of eternity. This is how a different evaluation could be opened up: in the fact that there is no value besides what has absolute value.

This different evaluation must also proceed from what Nietzsche was perhaps close to understanding: adoration has no object and consists precisely in not having any object. This can be understood doubly: not addressing itself to anything, and having nothing facing it. Not addressing itself to anything, to any being [être] or being [étant], and thus addressing *nothing*, this minimal *res* (this "sweet nothing") that is "reality" (not the majestic and overimposing Real of all ontotheologies): the *nothing* of the simple "here you are" [*voici*], "this is my body." But addressing itself to this *nothing*, insofar as it is infinitesimal—fortuitous, in-significant, and thus an *actual infinitude* (opposed to its potential in-finity, to the endlessness of *potentia* as such)—flashes as the signal of an absolute *outside*, of a *nihil* in which all nihilism loses its "-ism" (its supposed completion without further reference) in order to open infinitely onto a non-completion delivered from any horizon of accomplishment. Addressing itself, therefore, to this outside which cannot be said "as such."

As for having nothing facing it: neither as an object for a subject, nor as an objection to a thesis, nor as an objective to aim at. Therefore having the *nothing* of the infinitesimal-fortuitous-insignificant. Moreover, not having this infinitesimal-infinite thing *facing it*. Precisely not: it cannot face because there is no space that could be polarized according to a topology of the face-to-face. There is space turned in every part toward an outside that it does not face and that inhabits it rather than encountering it. That traverses it rather than surrounding it.

～

"L. responds that he is thinking about nothing.

Impossible, she must translate:

the thing—nothing [rien] rebus real reify republic revendication—he is thinking about the thing."[8]

    "I suffer easily, I suffer at the drop of a hat. Sometimes for nothing. Often for nothing because for me nothing is already something; something that cannot be described but that exists. When I try to explain this, everyone laughs at me."[9]

Intimacy

Unity in itself, intimacy without outside: by taking its fill of concentration, penetration, gathering in, and meditation (rumination, interminable return to the sole, fundamental impossibility of grasping "itself"), it becomes itself an *outside* and even an opening, then an exit, excess, generosity, or heroism, and then still later, abandon, escape, and even alienation, exclusion, exile.

    But this takes place according to an unceasing persistence, in the bosom of values that are too often posed unilaterally, those of the absolutely one and intimate: what is absolutely one and intimate constantly affirms and intensifies itself in this movement to the outside, outside itself, outside everything.

    To begin with: intimacy is always above all and perhaps always in absolute terms intimacy with an other, an intimacy among intimacies, and not the intimacy of one with herself alone. The intimate, the superlative of the "interior" (we have already quoted Augustine's address to God: "interior intimo meo"), is a superlative that, in itself, still calls for a comparative. Because I am filled up with interiority, at the closest proximity to "myself"—and most secretly—to "this world," to "the earth," I touch on something further: on what touches me out of an elsewhere that I can consider indifferently as "in" me or "outside" me, as within this world or outside it, because I am touching the limit. But to touch the limit is inevitably also to pass it. And I pass it only by touching another—another person, another being, another living being, even a hard stone, whose opaque resistance carries me yet further outside myself.

    All intimacy is "interior intimo meo." Being the most profound, it is also what, for its part, is bottomless. For Augustine and in the long tradition beginning with him, "God" will have been the name of what is bottomless. To touch the bottomless is to touch what allows itself to be touched only in retreating further still—in a hyperbole, in effect, of the law of touching, which says that one can only touch across a gap. Otherwise, one penetrates, but one can penetrate only what has some substance: here there is nothing of the sort, there is the incommensurability of this flight of the bottom to the outside, to the absolute elsewhere.

This touching is what one calls "spiritual": the breath that lightly brushes what is *"origin-heterogeneous* [hétérogène à l'origine]."[10] Spirit comes and touches this outside, which is further "outside" than any coupled assemblage of "inside/outside": it is even outside the outside. It is outside everything: it is nothing, which is to say, the reality of all things considered in itself, in absolute terms, which is to say, detached from everything. But a thing considered in absolute terms—as, perhaps, a musical chord, a nuance of color, an inflection of voice, a visage, a pebble, a tree— absorbs into this "nothing" the totality of consideration, whose spirit is then transported into this thing and changed into a sound, a color, a gaze or a smooth opacity. Such is adoration: the intimacy of this transport.

Being/Relation/Fervor

En diapheron eautō (the one differing [*différant*] from itself):[11] such is relation, insofar as it "is" or as "being" can designate anything beyond the One in-different in itself—which, truly, can be only by resonating as the verb *to be* [*être*] and not as a noun, *being* [*l'être*]. This, which Heidegger revealed, thereby initiating the deconstruction of ontology, has constantly preyed upon thought. Hegel says clearly that the one is its own negation, just as he says that being pure and simple abolishes itself as soon as it is posed. But what is Descartes himself doing, when he pronounces "I am," other than opening a "being" that is neither substance nor position, but enunciation and declaration—what's more, a declaration whose verb cannot exist without its subject, a subject inscribed in it in the form of "am" but also detached as "I," a pronoun that is nothing other than the difference of the "am" from itself, the possibility that it might present, declare, and designate itself?[12] "I am" is already in relation, if only in the relation of withdrawal from the rest of the world. This withdrawal is not at all solipsistic or closed off: on the contrary, it opens relation. "I" is a relation to the world, to others, to "you," to "us." It is also a relation to its proper being, which it only "is" insofar as it relates to it—but it relates only insofar as it relates to all the rest (a "thinking being" means one that feels, imagines, wants, conceives, loves). There is hardly a question of "consciousness" here, or of the "subject" as a depository of representations. It is a question of placing in relation.

The subject as subject of a relation—we should say subject *in* a relation—is itself according to the relation. Thus it is unity via its difference, the unity of a tension and a rhythm, a unity that is mobile in itself and whose mobility creates tension, drive, aspiration, contradiction, opposition, loss and pardon, alliance and rupture, opening and closing. Deferring [*différant*] in itself, different [*différent*] from itself and differing [*différant*] itself: opening itself as a voice, as a mouth.

Exclaiming. "I adore," "I adore you [*t'adore*]," "I adore you [*vous*]" are exclamations. A free-for-all of acclaim [*Mêlée d'acclamation*]. But without clamor. It can be proffered noiselessly just as well as dramatically. It can efface itself in order to slip completely into a proper name, whose meaning then becomes "since you are there!" Perhaps the name "god," coming in place of all the names of the gods, came to concern the pure beating of exclamation. The beat of beating itself, one could say, the redoubling of erotic impetus, of amorous love, of the invocation of all sorts of greatness, beauty, and transport—transports the beat itself. "God" could be understood as "what joy!" or "what grandeur!"—a salutation to the incommensurable not designating any sort of being, designating only itself as salutation. But this is a surprised salutation, caught in speech by surprise, lower than any formulation [*phrase*], borne by voice rather than speech stricto sensu, a nomination of the unnamable or of what is namable par excellence—through excess, through the profusion hidden within each name. A salutation of pure resonance, carrying salutation to *jouissance*, to a joying [*jouir*] that joys in saying or in being said.

Religions were full of exclamations—hallelujah, evoe, hosannah, om, Jesus, Allah . . . —exclamations that overflow any sense the words bearing them might have had. It always involves a voice that clamors, exclaims, acclaims, and thus proclaims. But it does not declaim or demand anything. If this is what is meant by "religious sentiment," then we are far from religion as observance and belief. We are simply, if one can say so, in the realm of emotion—the emotion of infinite relation. Of course, this emotion can be exploited, and doubtless all cultures know such exploitation, which becomes the business of priests, gurus, and sorcerers. Of itself, emotion is as ready to submit as to exalt itself, and thus it gives a handle for religious manipulation as we know it only too well (not to speak of the traffic that ensures when emotion is accompanied by a demand for salvation . . .). However, this is not a sufficient reason to hold the fervor of adoration in suspicion and to class it as illusion: the dis-enclosure of reason also has to open toward a fervor.

The various fascisms were not deceived about this, and it was not by chance that they had recourse to emotion: not only did they know what force it made available, but they knew that this force was seeking to discharge itself, seeking expression in a world that it experienced as dessicated. In Greek, "enthusiasm" means "passage to god" or "sharing the divine": How can enthusiasm be saved from the death of God? This is a serious question.

We should begin by not confusing the fervor of enthusiasm with fascistic fury: the latter is always concerned with a determinate, closed figure (whether people or party, leader or idea, vision or conception). A configured, closed figure without an outside. It is received as such, full, circumscribed, accomplished: one submits to it. This is adulation, not adoration. The fervor of adoration, by contrast, is given by choice [*élection*], in the dilection whereby a unique, priceless price is agreed upon and/or recognized. The fervor that choice carries with it does not simply carry a single loved being to the incandescence of an absolute. At the same time, and without contradiction, this fervor desires this incandescence for everything (all beings). It is a fervor for multiple and singular existence: for each one, therefore, in turn, for each one excluding all others, and yet also for all, at least for the many who respond to the many modes of this unique and polymorphous "love."

Passage

"God" could be the name that, as a proper noun [*nom*], names the unnamable and, as a common noun, designates the division *dies/nox*, day and night, opening the rhythm of the world, the possibility of distinctions in general, and therefore of relation and of passage.

But we can erase this sign if it begins to dominate, take control, subjugate: it then becomes contradictory, in effect, as it annuls passage, annuls us as passers-by, attempts to fix us permanently before altars, temples, books. This is what happens, perhaps unavoidably, in all the theological and metaphysical determinations of "God," and it is perhaps impossible for this name, as for any other, not to be determined in some way. It is perhaps impossible for this name to retain the movement, the trembling of the gap and the passage.

"God" should only be named in passing, and as a passer-by.

Man: the pace [*pas*] of the passer-by in whom the world surpasses all its limits or conditions: the beginning and the end, the limit and the unlimited, unity and dispersion, totality and particularity. This step beyond [*pas au-delà*] is the doing of *sense*—or *language*—which is, in all of its forms, a referring [*renvoi*] to the outside. Man is the being of sense: he is through and through a *referring*.

Exceeding all conditions, without its own condition (the "human condition" is beyond conditions), man is the unconditioned: at once without condition, without conditioning, without determination, and absolute, constituting a sovereign principle, demand, and commandment. But this is the sovereignty of nothing, or of passage.

Passage and referring are themselves indefinitely multiplied—as are the senses (the five, and all the others, whether electric, magnetic, kinetic . . .), and as are the "senses" of the word *sense*—precisely because this concerns referring: each register refers to the outside, to what lies outside everything and is formed both by the very ensemble of referrings and by the complete suspension of all referring.

Thus knowledge and imagination, language and sensation, sex and childbirth, technology and nature, solitude and relation are so many registers that are at once crossing one another and heterogeneous. Nothing is taken up into a totality. This is precisely what invites adoration: what unfurls rather than gathers back in.

Adoration: a gesture recognizing a passage that infinitely surpasses, passes beyond. Therefore a gesture recognizing that there can be no recognition proper of infinite surpassing. To recognize an infinite is to finitize it, to de-fine it. What is at stake here is the recognition of what cannot be recognized. And of the fact that it obliges me to bow down. In bowing down, I open the finite to the infinite.

"Adoration" makes us think of "prostration." Prostration is formidably ambiguous: it attests to the incommensurability of that before which it prostrates itself, and it allows this abasement to be exploited: the permanent little scheme of religions. But religion—let us say, the religious, observant disposition—is finally alone in opening the possibility of prostration. Perhaps we should see here the sense of Hegel's phrase, that "religion must remain for all, including those for whom it has been elevated to a concept." The philosopher, he who understands in conceptual terms the truth that only religion represents, knows how to do everything except prostrate himself. This follows from there being for him neither god nor master: this is the condition of thinking. Yet the philosopher must prostrate himself: *as a philosopher*, he must know that reason prostrates itself before what in itself surpasses it infinitely. He therefore needs to know that only a reason that adores is fully rational and reasonable. Kant prostrates himself: "Two things awe me most, the starry sky above me and the moral law within me." By this we are to understand that the starry sky and the moral law are two names for the infinite opening of reason.

Thus one never prostrates oneself before "something" or before "someone." One does not adore something or someone—no more than one is properly the subject or the agent of one's adoration—rather, it always involves opening as movement and passage, or the infinite insofar as it is transitive: as it transfixes [*transit*] us.

Sense: not the sending [*envoi*] of a signification to an addressee, but sending as making sense, carrying it off with it, displacing it—sense always displaced, being displaced. A passer-by, a passenger, furtive insofar as it is fortuitous. Always a sign made in passing, a "salut!" Therefore always also interrupted, incomplete: a failure of sense (in the weighty sense full of significance) alone renders possible the lightness demanded by sending, referring [*renvoi*], the passage of sense in its aerial sense of breath, of palpable, sensual light contact, which is always a little senseless.

In this failure also lodges the possible impulse to an insurrection: a refusal of the given world, an impetus to alter this world (not to transform it but to break it open), an affirmation of another (of the) world *here and now*.

Economy

The mutation from which monotheism and Christianity issued was a mutation of civilization in the fullest sense of the word (of this word produced par excellence by this "civilization"): mutation in its manner and sense of presence in the world. A metamorphosis in how one inhabited the world—without doubt the third great mutation after that of the Neolithic age and that of Empires—a transformation of the *oikos*, of the house (dwelling, hearth, kin, domesticity) and of its running, *oikonomia*. The Mediterranean world enters into a new economy—commercial, monetary, entrepreneurial, and expansive—which, after a delay (or incubation?) of several centuries, took on its full dimensions with the Renaissance.

This aspect of the mutation closely corresponds to what has been characterized as the passage from a culture of observance to a culture of relation. "Correspondence" does not imply any unilateral determination—neither of economy by the sphere of representations and institutions nor, conversely, of this sphere by economy. One can clearly see, in their transformation, how these spheres or registers belong to one another in a tight, symbiotic way and signal above all their belonging to a general schema of one "civilization" rather than another. These schemata take shape in the most secret depths of human history, in an invisible movement that is neither progressive nor regressive, but simply metamorphic. This history has no sense, no directing or orienting sense, apart from the sense of finally having been brought to the point of laying bare the concern for "sense" itself.

The schema of reproduction gave way to the schema of production. Reproduction does not simply involve consecrating wealth to maintaining given conditions, but at the same time reproduces a way of life and the life of observances and hierarchies.[13] As was stated above, here violence and riches—always linked—are turned toward glorious possession. By contrast, in the regime of production they are turned toward fruitful possession. What is to be produced no longer lies, by definition, within given conditions but surpasses them, deranges them, carries them off. In the place of life, observance, and hierarchy are produced existence, enterprise, and law—or rather, they are at once subjects and objects of production—three forms or three dimensions offered straightaway in the element of becoming, of transformation, of the in-finite. This is how one enters into what can be called in the most general terms *relation*.

Before the regime of production is truly deployed in the Renaissance, and thus in the contemporaneous deployment of relation (society in its modern concept—or problem: credit, the cost of risk, organization, transport, exploration, etc.), there are two intermediate stages, both marked by a singular relation to religion. The first is Antiquity, which started off "pre-capitalism," but within the framework, maintained for a while, of "civil religion," an observance that eventually was revealed to be powerless to account for this world in transformation. Following after it, feudalism, which is not a Mediterranean but a Nordic configuration, seemed to return to reproduction, but within a framework still defined by the distinction between two worlds or two kingdoms. While the feudal system was closely tied up with Christian practices, the division between the seigneury of the world and the seigneury of the heavens remained clear.

The production of existence leads to that of the subject and of the individual—of he who is supposed to be the subject of his own interests. One could say that the schema of production opens onto a new problematic of the "proper" in general: of property, whether private or collective,[14] but also of the property/ies of the more and more autonomous techniques of production (from enterprise to industry, to the machine, then to cybernetics and IT), and at the same time of the rights of property or appropriation—those of society, of the State, of the regime designated as that of "human rights," which supposes a possible (and yet unlocatable) determination of what the "human" properly is.

This ensemble of the "proper," expanding or indefinitely in flight—which also becomes the ensemble of the proper "needs" and proper "ends" that a civilization can or should offer—started off the process of what is called unlimited "growth," which corresponds to an increase in what we ("we," the very actors and instruments of the process) can only consider as expropriations or disappropriations (of goods, cultures, or identities), as what "alienates" us or gets us stuck in the "inauthentic."

Today we know how this growth runs up against, not only the objections and anxiety occasioned by a general feeling that the only proper thing remaining to us is to serve a process that is assumed to be autonomous and irreversible—and with this service, this servitude, to accept an unlimited domination by profit, which has become the essential object of production—but also ecological imbalances, the depletion of nonrenewable resources, and the formidable complexity of technical possibilities in medicine, in space exploration, in the control of bodies and minds, and in the transformation of cultures, to say nothing of financial manipulations.

The necessity of taking back or taking up a regulatory and interventionary authority over this "growth" is undeniable. It obliges us to invent or alter codes, institutions, guidelines. As has often been repeated, we must make capitalism "moral." But this morality, understood as that of the individual and the entirety of his interests—as the morality that is proper to a "man" whose metaphysical situation, as it were, remains unchanged—has every chance of remaining powerless, since it either proceeds from the same point as the problem itself, namely, "man" as de jure individual-producer-subject . . . , or, in its revolutionary form, brings us back to the presupposition, merely in a less clearly determined way, that "man" is a given. Marx thinks the "total man" as the integral, non-alienated producer of his own social and individual existence, but this pure production value (which in Marx in fact underpins the very idea of "value," in the pure sense that it attempts to oppose to market value) covers over and obliterates the simple question: *What* man, what humanity ought to be produced?

When one turns toward a form of regulation interior to capitalism, as today it is doubtless necessary for us to do—for instance, the form best represented by Keynes—the same question reappears in a different form. Here is an strong, courageous affirmation by Keynes, which has a lively resonance today:

> I see us free, therefore, to return to some of the most sure and certain principles of religion and traditional virtue—that avarice is a

vice, that the exaction of usury is a misdemeanour, and the love of money is detestable, that those walk most truly in the paths of virtue and sane wisdom who take least thought for the morrow. We shall once more value ends above means and prefer the good to the useful. We shall honour those who can teach us how to pluck the hour and the day virtuously and well, the delightful people who are capable of taking direct enjoyment in things, the lilies of the field who toil not, neither do they spin.[15]

The evangelical reference could be analyzed at length, insofar as it invokes the Judeo-Christian—and philosophical—relation to money, but let us leave that to one side and ask: When this reference is just a memory (as it must be for Keynes), how can the "direct enjoyment in things" be sketched with any precision? How, in general terms, can the "ends" and the "good," which everyone agrees must be preferred to the "means" and the "useful," be determined? This questioning comment does not contain the least irony: I only want to underline how Keynes, just as much as Marx or anyone else—so far as I know—who could be called upon with the aim of transforming the economy, shows very clearly that we should not start with the economy itself or with its regulation, but with "ends," or rather, "sense"—let us therefore say simply with metaphysics, or, if one prefers, with the terms *mysticism* or *poetics*. But whichever name one chooses, we must start with the work of thinking through these names, this regime of names, the relation to infinite sense.

Doubtless what is called the "market" should be set right [*régler*], regularized, and regulated. However, so long as it is seen in these terms, we will remain subject to a play of forces that must be controlled. This play depends upon a profound choice, ungraspable in itself, of "civilization," just as "capitalism" and "industry" depended upon underground, secular, anonymous movements, whose thrust defied any prescription of consciousness and even of "reason." We can no longer decide consciously and reasonably on a choice that could reverse or overturn the previous one—a choice that is perhaps already at work, unknown to us. It is not a question of preaching voluntarism. It is a question of making oneself as little unsuited as possible to perceiving and receiving the tectonic shudderings that are rocking "civilization."

This means that we must admit with Heidegger that "humanism does not set the *humanitas* of man high enough"[16]—a *humanitas* that, on the contrary, has ended up being thought as the essence of a subject of interests and rights in place of being turned toward the non-essence of an "eksistence"—and distance ourselves from the thinking of the same Heidegger when it more or less expressly refers the "inspection" [*arraisonnement*] of the world[17] to an "oblivion" (whether we say "of being" or of something else matters little here), what we should be learning to think is that nothing is forgotten, nothing is lost, no authenticity of the world or of mankind has been alienated, but rather that the reason of "inspection" must be dis-enclosed.

Does this mean that, as Heidegger said, "only a god can save us"? Undoubtedly, we must understand instead the divinity of this "god," on the one hand, and, on the other, no longer speak of "salvation" (saving, *Rettung*), but learn how to salute, to salute one another, as we have already seen.[18]

Everyone/Fulfillment [*le comble*]

A condition of adoration: anteriority to "I"; not simply to "me" and its masses (the masses that a "me" is and the masses of "me's"), but also to "I" itself and to its punctual location, which remains a position nonetheless, though fleeting and without dimension. This takes place further upstream: the opening opens behind me, before I open my mouth. "I" could happen in this opening, but does not yet appear, not for the moment; there is only the circle or ellipsis of the mouth, which has not yet spoken, which precedes not only the sound of words but silent intention, too. The sense of adoration is not to be found in intention, or perhaps we should say, taking up Derrida's analysis, that it carries intention to the point where it is abandoned: it is stretched out by the desire to let go—to cry out—but this very desire is carried, paradoxically thrust forward by an abandon, not a renunciation but an intimate trust and assent—*interior intimo* . . . —given to a movement older and broader than subjectivity and identity.

It is not me and it is not even "one" who adores. Everyone passing through this one and this "everyone" gradually designates a contact, a contagion of all beings. This "everyone" is no assembly or social bond, but neither is it an organic or fusional incorporation. It is a "with" that is experienced and known in a proximity that is neither exterior (like "bond" or "relationship") nor interior (like symbiosis or absorption). It is what I am in the eyes of an attentive other, or what a form or color—of a tree, a tool—is when I allow it to enter and go through me, to not remain before me.

It is less a "relation without relation" than relation itself, in absolute terms, as opening and passage, but above all as opening and passage affect and touch what [*cela*] is open and toward which things [*ça*] pass.[19] This concerns above all what opens affect in general: a receptivity, passivity, or capacity for sensation that must already be given, and given as already open, in order for something like affection to take place. Receptivity—sensibility, excitability—is nothing other than the plurality of existences and the real heterogeneity between them that is the corollary of the absence of another world or world beyond, where an ultimate homogeneity would hold sway. Beings affect one another—even minerals do—and the world, or the sense of the world, is nothing other than the general communication of this emotion: the shaking of creation.

If adoration, in this communication, abolishes relationship [*relation*] without turning into fusion—or effusion . . .—if it exceeds both relation and non-relation in the sense of identification, assimilation (devouring, absorption, etc.), perhaps one can say that it touches the *fulfillment* [comble] of relation: where it realizes, exposes, or delivers its *sense*.

Sense as a fulfilling [*comblement*]. The sense of adoration as a fulfilling of its impetus, its movement, its desire.

Roland Barthes dares to talk about the *fulfillment* of love. He dares to think, posit, and, as he says, risk this serious infringement of the psychoanalytical *doxa* of a necessary lack. In any case, as he says, he dares to *try* to do so. This trying, as he also says, is that of love. It is what young love (or love insofar as it is young) tries to do: to fill and to be filled.

Which is to say, to overflow. One might well begin with lack, a gap to fill, as Barthes does, but one proceeds, as he knows, toward overflowing. In this fulfillment is deployed a logic of filling up [*comble*]: an extremity that surpasses, insofar as it surpasses. The issue is no longer that of a lack to be filled, but rather of a desire that overflows. This is, after all, the essence of desire, of the pleasure that desire gathers to itself, to its infinite setting back into play.

Such is *jouissance*, or rather joying, *jouir*: not a state but an act, and an act that overflows itself. Not a satisfaction, as if the hollow that is filled up were cancelled out, not even a saturation—even though what is saturated always exudes what saturates and overflows it. But something that would be like the expansion of the hollow beyond its filling up, and thanks to this fulfillment. It is not that lack always outlasts what sates it. But the hollow, in being filled up, reveals how it is not lack but power: the capacity to welcome in order to desire anew. It is not yawning emptiness, but opening, call, impetus.

Thinking doesn't happen any differently; it affirms what exceeds any power of thinking. It affirms itself, in effect, as the power of its very powerlessness. It knows to think that there is something it cannot think: not only that nothing greater can be thought, but that there is still a thought greater than all that can be thought. This is Anselm's argument, which another *doxa* made into an ontological proof. But what exceeds thought is neither a being [*être*], nor of being [*de l'être*]. Doubtless, it "is" not. This is why the supposed ontological proof falls down so easily, even as what "is" not carries thought further onward.

What gives a film its power, grandeur, and beauty is not on the screen. It breaks through the screen. It is the desire, the love carried by the film, which is precisely what allows one to speak of the film otherwise than as an object, a work, or a production.

The process of filling up operates at once as an overflowing and a withdrawal: art, or love, is poured out there and then gathered back again, more tightly, more rigorously. Joying becomes ascetic, a meditation on the essential, a thought of what does not allow itself to be thought. A joy of knowing that one is before what is ever greater.

Overflowing need not be either a ferment or a disgorging. It can simply, imperceptibly, surpass the brim, as water completely filling up a cup forms a slight bulge, a thin convergent meniscus that rises higher than the edges of the glass. The filling up trembles, it is fragile.[20]

This fragility is that of the "sense of the world [that] must lie outside the world."[21]

Spirit?

How are we to name the regime or the register according to which "adoration" is to be conceived? It is quite clear that this is not politics.[22] Neither are we in the arena of morality, ethics, or aesthetics: instead the point seems to be, in relation to these categories, to exceed their boundaries. Nor are we in the arena of philosophy, since the register is one of conduct rather than of reflection and analysis. We find ourselves visibly in a space that everything today would lead us to call "spiritual," using a term that reappears slowly and timidly, as a bruised survivor of spiritualist effusions and masquerades. In these very pages I have used this word several times. But it nonetheless remains difficult, it continues to weigh us down, because we still hear there the tone of its idealist or mystical unction.

What threatens the lexicon of spirit is an overdetermination based on "breath" [*souffle*], despite what it tells us about respiration—rhythm, inspiration, expiration—we fear that the word might still be attached to the image of a sort of magical breath [*haleine*], with which it might inflate anew the values of a pneumaticism (which does not mean that I take back what I said earlier about the "holy spirit"). Thinking about breath alone leads toward immediate, inarticulate, and, as it were, inaudible exhalation.

But in "adoration" the voice chimes. Which is to say, speech or song do, and in them, before or beyond signification, sense as call, address, and therefore also as relation. The relation of a "salut!"

For there is relation, there is only that. Its terms matter fairly little—whether they be based on content or subjects of knowledge or representation, whether they be "men" or other beings—and only the relation that is divided/shared, in both senses of the word *partage*, between all the world's existents, matters. An infinite relation that does not relate anything—no senses caught in a net—and that opens everything and everyone. An infinite relation that only finitude knows.

ᘯ

Adoration is stretched out toward things and by them. Stretched out [*tendue*] without intention. Phenomenological intentionality toward the world is replaced by—or joined to, it comes down to the same thing—an extension toward the outside. Or rather: an extension of the inside, its dilatation, sometimes to the point of exasperation and rupture. To that of death. But also to that of the excess of life, to excessive life.

Opening, expansion, dis-enclosure: the world dis-enclosed, unmade [*défait*], delivered, un-worlded.

This is the deployment and (perhaps) the leading astray of the *as if*. Relation to an inexistent, mimesis without model.

This is a relation to an inexistent because there is nothing to be reached: not that it is the "void" or an infinite flight, but simply that what is involved, what is "adored," is not "something," is not a "being" [*être*] (or a "being" [*étant*]). Adoration goes toward the faraway as such, toward a distancing that is not distance from an object, from a goal, but the distancing that adoration itself creates, that it opens. I do not adore "someone" or some "work." But I adore, and thus a distancing that is properly the expansion of adoration opens up. It does not put at a distance "the" person or "the" thing adored: it carries them off into this distancing that distances us infinitely from one another and *that also distances everyone from himself.*

Distance here does not mean a distance between two points (subjects or objects). Its value is as an opening or a distention that places things beyond reach. That removes the possibility of designating points, subjects, objects, or distances. Distancing simply distances those who are close, those who are the closest, and thus opens the incommensurable.

In truth, adoration is addressed to distancing, it turns toward the faraway, because this faraway renders all proximity possible.

Complements, Supplements, Fragments ■ *87*

But this faraway remains at a distance, leaves us to our fragility. There is something of the inexorable, and adoration cannot change into exoration. It is no accident that the God of the monotheisms is called "merciful": one expects him to be exorable to our imploring. But adoration does not ask for that. It carries imploring within it, or rather, deploration: we are pitiful—but adoration recognizes that this state of misery is not a degeneration. Instead it is the condition of being abandoned in a fortuitous world. This abandonment hides within it both weakness and strength, finitude and infinitude intertwined. Thus the "salut!" is exchanged without any call to be saved—and, in being exchanged, it also presents what keeps us "virtuous": not renouncing our impetus, our desire, without thinking that we can assuage them, either. Accepting that they always open us anew.

The Faraway: Death

Dear Hugo,[23]

So to have faith is to believe in something lying beyond death.

I can go along with this. One can only have faith in what exceeds all possibilities of grasping by reason and by whatever sense it might be.

Above all, I would like to recall that faith is not belief. Not in its essence, at least, as this difference turns out to be complicated. Belief is a weak faith, a sort of supposition, a projection to which one adheres not by proof but because one needs to put up a show of knowledge where none can be found. Faith is trust, and trust in the strongest sense, which is to say, a trust that cannot ultimately be explained or justified. A trust that is justified is assured [assurée], guaranteed: it is not really "trust." And yet all trust is somehow justified, because otherwise there would be no reason to trust one thing rather than another: but the ultimate perspective of this logic remains that of an absence of reason(s) . . .

Faith is holding to an assurance about which nothing is sure, which can be neither perceived nor comprehended. Belief is an assurance that somehow gives itself a perception or quasi-perception and quasi-comprehension of the "reason" for my assurance. Belief therefore comes down to a representation, even if it is indistinct, hazy, badly determined. Faith, strictly speaking, does not rely on any representation at all.

Death is that whereof there is no possible representation. In it the "subject of representation" disappears: in it, "I" disappear. In it, the other who disappears withdraws beyond any way in which I might be able to reach "him," that is, the "I" that he was when alive. *The* dead person [le *mort*] can indeed be represented—in memories, via the presence of a corpse: but in both cases, only representation is before me and not the "I" of the other.[24]

In *Noli me tangere*,[25] since that's where your letter begins, I tried to say two things, which in truth the book does not sufficiently distinguish from one another.

The first: in insisting on the meaning of *anastasis*, which comes from Hebrew, and on the "raising" of the body, I wanted to set up an opposition to resurrection as rebirth, regeneration, a new beginning to life, which is to say, to the representation of a simple beginning anew in "another life." For this "other life," represented in this way, is only the projection of this life, the one that has been lived by the dead person, or, in my own case, that I am now living. Broadly, this projection is hallucination (it goes in the direction of the phantom, the apparition, etc.). In opposition to this, I wanted to index resurrection as a tipping up [*basculement*] of *sense*: the horizontal of the dead body tips up to the vertical. The dead person is not living once more, but the sense of his life—namely, his sense, the sense of being "I" swerves: instead of continuing to "go toward," it stops, rises up, becoming at once the ultimate end and completed representation of this "sense of being me." In such a representation, which is at the same time a closure, and a closure lacking the possibility of being legitimized as an "accomplishment" (even when one can say that this was a rich life, "lived to the full," etc.), the following presents itself: that the sense of "being me" itself has no sense. That it does not undergo any assumption or raising up as part of a sense that would be global, divine, and so on, but that it makes sense or is sense in just this way: not by being infused with a grand cosmic signification, but by being kept at a distance, separated, within the crisp contours of its completed "life."

This is what Heidegger names the "possibility of impossibility" and the "highest possibility" of existence. But as Derrida shows, this possibility undermines itself as a possibility; it cannot even be grasped as "possible," let alone appropriated as the "highest possibility," in the way that Heidegger's discourse renders it completely appropriable. There is an expropriation by way of principle, which can be stated simply: I remain without access to my own death, just as I have no access to that of the other insofar as he is an "I" (i.e., insofar as he is, strictly speaking, an other to me). Purely and simply, without access. In other words, "the sense of 'being has no sense itself'" is an untenable proposition because it annuls the sense of "sense."

Nonetheless, I persist in saying that in "comprehending" sense in this way—as relation to or dispatching toward an annulment of "sense"—we can touch on something, without for all that "acceding," and therefore without "comprehending," either. Holding oneself in this relation without comprehension, without conclusion, without representation, deprived of sense, therefore also within this relation to "I" (whether my own or another's), insofar as it is deprived of sense or is an eclipse of itself, is all that we can name "faith" insofar as it supposes the annulment of all kinds of knowledge and representation.

This was what the tipping up to the vertical axis (which was followed in *Noli me tangere* by the Ascension, by departure without return) meant, above all.

But I also know that "this" is entirely dependent on the discourse of which it is a part, which articulates it. And that this discourse is nothing next to death, to the pain, even the horror, of death (once again, my own or that of others). This remains a thought in the irresistibly "abstract" or immaterial sense of the word. I am not looking for any path of consolation that would reintroduce representations, assurances of a return to life, and so on, but for a point where thought—which I am convinced is material, palpable, concrete—and the experience of fright, anguish, and dereliction before death, whether mine or that of others, might come into contact.

A contact point: here we come back to "do not touch me." I ought to have realized this and developed this further. But it was underlying, half-conscious . . .

In any case, the second intention or field of resonance of what I was attempting is: that the same thought—let us say, that of the impossible or of sense eclipsed—is also, can only also be thought as palpable, sentiment, sensation itself. It brings with it a sort of perception, which, however, is not the hallucinatory perception of the phantom—since hallucination is the end of thought. This perception is not of death or of the dead person. As soon as I name the dead person—whether me or another—he is removed from the abstraction of death [*"la" mort*] (of "this unreality," to speak like Hegel). I begin to grant him another life: not another life in another world, but the other of life in the world of the living, and therefore still a life. The life of the dead—finally, what a good number of beliefs have set up and staged in all sorts of cultures. (And doubtless here the limits, crossings, and contacts between cultures are also at issue).

Now, we like to give life to the dead, to think that they are present, as we like to think that we could be present beyond our own death. (It isn't the same thing, but for the moment let us keep them together.) But this is not simply to make "them" live, this is not simply a representation. Or rather, this touches on a region that I am unable to name, that seems to me to be suspended between representation, thought, sentiment, and sensation. For this life of the dead is at the same time their non-life, the pure ceasing of their being as "I," *and* the life whose imprint is in us and continues living there with a life that cannot be reduced to representation. This life is what I know and feel of the presence, allure, and voice of a dead person and is a true trace of him, a living trace incorporated in me. And this is why it is so hard to feel this presence and its complete absence at the same time.

Here I am no longer within faith as I have defined it. Not that I am in belief as weak knowledge. Or rather: I am between pure thought and representation. I am in a sensibility that, in the final analysis, is perhaps neither strictly speaking mine nor that of the dead person (who feels nothing any longer) but is the sensibility of our meeting, of what we lived through together (which can be stretched to more than one meeting, to more than one "whole," but with all the differences in intensity and intimacy of these encounters).

Perhaps one should not think death without also thinking the dead, or perhaps one should not submit the dead entirely to death. Just as—and this "just as" is not only analogical, it is real—they are well and truly in the world, in molecules or in atoms caught up in different combinations, different crystallizations; they are also in the community, if I dare to put this word forward. I mean the community that shares this small part of being that is the contingency of the world. This community is nothing other, if you will, than what Freud names the id, which is ultimately the common part of the unconscious. Under this name or another, or without any name, what is at stake is what links us together, indeed, not only us humans but the totality of beings—the animal within us, and even the vegetable, the mineral . . .

Everything is played out here around individuation: death is individual; it is not equal to the totality of being [*l'étant*] (this is indeed Spinoza, and the question is perhaps that of finding a new Spinozism . . .). But the dead person, for his part, is neither an individual nor a simple pulverization of molecules via the totality of being [*l'étant*]. The living individual is never simply the individual *stricto sensu*, closed off in his independence. He is also—"I" am, in each moment—made up of all the relations of which I am a part, from my sensations to my thoughts, passing through my friendships, my readings, and so on, my entire imaginary and all that makes "sense." Can we think that the dead person lives on with such a life, yet without representing the seat of an "I" and its relation to self?

To think this is to be concerned with representation, therefore with belief, and even with imagination—with fantasy, if you will, with the phantasm—but at the same time it proceeds from both thought and the experience of life. In any case, thought must not refuse to approach what, being only illusion with regard to all that we can posit about the real, nonetheless says something true: at least this, that the plurality of *relation* does not die.

For relation is at stake here. My mother once told me, by way of ending a conversation on resurrection several years after the death of my father: "Allow me to think that there is a place where I shall find him again." She was right, since she was not implying that this place was a place within the space of the world or even in a beyond-space extrapolated from that of the world. A completely different place, but a place. (Perhaps the one Jacques indicated by saying "I love you and I am smiling at you from wherever I might be"—which implied "wherever" and perhaps "nowhere" and yet an "I might be".[26]) A place and a being *as a place and a being of relation, of encounter or a happy encounter.*

Of course, the dead are definitively, irreversibly, and unbearably absent, and more than absent: disappeared, abolished. Of course, no work of mourning ever reduces this abolition. Yet if we do not sink into melancholy, which is to die in our turn in the midst of life—becoming one of the living dead but not rejoining the life of the dead person for all that, instead petrifying our relation to him—we live, we survive "our dead" (as one says), and this cannot be reduced to an egotistical instinct. It is the continuation of relation, and it can be the awaiting and the approach of a happy encounter in an unheard-of place and according to an unknown mode of being.

Insofar as I think it is important to keep faith apart from belief, I think one can say that. It does not proceed from an illusion or from an assurance in the complete absence of any representation. And what passes between the two regimes is concerned with affect, not with the concept. And affect is relation, one could say.

Now you are going to ask me: What about *my own death*? You will perhaps reproach me for placing all the emphasis on the side of the other's death. It's true. But I have done so because, ultimately, it seems that my death can only be envisaged in the terms whereby I envisage that of others. At the same time it is true, with Heidegger, that in my death "I" disappear in such a way that it is not even "mine," and it is true to insist, as Blanchot did, on the absolute inappropriability of my death and on the unending churning of the *dying* [*le* mourir] whereby I am constantly taking leave of myself or making sense absent, and absolutely so. But at the same time, and precisely apropos of Blanchot (one could also come back to Proust, to the death of Bergotte), if some people write—and others make films, compose, paint, and so on—it is in order to give form, always anew, to this: *that we communicate this dying to one another.* Which is to say, that we share the sense of the absence of sense and the relation to what has neither reason, nor end, nor assurance, meaning ultimately that we are all within faith and that we all communicate in it, without knowing it or wanting it.

(Here I am leaving aside how the works of those who write, compose, etc. communicate with those who do nothing of the sort and even with those who remain without relation to these "works." That is another matter, but one must emphasize that *there is communication*, and that there is communication always of the same relation to the without-reason-without-end, and therefore to death. The same relation of dying. Of course, one can find all that one can imagine attempting to deny or suppress this, to cover it up: all beliefs, superstitions, and enterprises of auto-suggestion. But finally, those who truly hallucinate are rare; the majority know without knowing the non-knowledge that makes up relation. Without which there would be no civilization, literature, music, etc.).

On the topic of my death, I can only replay the same counterpoint between faith and belief—yes, the same *fugue*, whose theme is precisely a flight that is infinite and without conclusion. This flight at once allows my thinking to be held in an affirmation of the eclipse of the "subject of sense" that "I" am, and allows my sensibility to feel the continuation of relation, of relations—the "awaiting one another" that Jacques talks about. To think, therefore, with a dreamy or naïve thought, but one that is also poetic—and this word should take on here all the power of which it is capable—the unheard-of place where my unheard-of being, which will no longer be "mine," *will be back among* "its own" [retrouvera *"les siens"*].

Ultimately, to think these things without entering into the embarrassment of a strange interweaving of reason and naïveté, or rather, without placing faith under the control of belief, one would have to say that "I" is not—that I am not—the only relation to me, punctual and separated (absolute in the strict sense), but that I am the totality of relations according to which only I can relate to myself, beginning, of course, with language (beginning, yet without establishing any order in stringing together language and gaze, gesture, and touch, all the feeling of the other beings, the other "I's," and the others who are not "I's" or do not bear witness to being so). This would be nothing more than to probe more seriously, I could almost say more gravely, than we normally do into all the thinking of the distance from self in the relation to self: the most pregnant being Jacques's, since *différance* responds to nothing other than this—with which one can also associate Deleuze and his "becoming-*x*" (animal, woman, imperceptible). These ways of thinking originated in Hegel on self-consciousness and alienation, whom Nietzsche follows with the illusion of the "subject," and doubtless Spinoza provides another model, anterior to subjectivity, in which "God," that is to say, the "totality of beings" [*totalité de l'étant*], consists precisely in "conceiving things under the aspect of eternity":[27] there, the relation to self is not indexed to identity, but to the pleasure or joy of knowledge according to an "aspect of eternity," a knowledge that is therefore also that of our own eternity and, indissociably, of our community with other men and with the rest of the world.

If Spinoza can say that "we feel and know from experience that we are eternal," that is because this experience is that of our relation, which is "to itself" only insofar as it is to the entirety of the rest of beings [*l'étant*] and thus to the incommensurable (which Spinoza names "God"), from which we can receive joy but which we cannot know. From this, one understands that "joy" here is not very different from "faith" as I think it should be understood. Or from what Spinoza names "intellectual love."

"Intellectual love," undoubtedly this cuts to the quick (if I dare say so) of the problem: How and at what point can we join together "love" and "intellect"? In contemporary terms, I would say: How, at what point, can we understand that the *différance* of identity is indeed a drive to and desire for the other (of an other, of all alterity)? If we are able to respond, then we are also able to reduce—a little . . .—the fracture between the possible thought of our eternity—or immortality—and the impossible sensation or affect of it. We would then also know how to surmount the opposition between faith and knowledge, which is to say, between faith and belief.

But we are incapable of doing this, which is why, when religious fervor no longer carries us along (supposing that it was ever capable of what is involved), all the thinking of which we are capable cannot remove anything, not a single atom, from the mourning for oneself and thus from the fear or terror in which we cannot avoid existing. I would not want what I have said to seem to be looking for a new form of consolation. But perhaps we need to go beyond consolation/desolation, in the same way that the sentiment or the sense of irreparable loss—the mourning that no work can resolve—lies beyond the couple melancholy/forgetting. For the sense of the irreparable can be joined to an affirmation of life that does not offer any reparation but that, in living, also continues to live with the dead and perhaps, in certain cases, for certain temperaments—or indeed secretly for everyone? . . .—to go toward them *both* now, in life, *and* later, in dying in our turn.

All of this, I know and I say it again, is untenable for both thinking and sensibility. An impossibility for one and an infinite sorrow for the other. But we conduct [*tenons*] ourselves, the immense majority of mankind conducts itself in this untenable situation.[28] This is not simply done by instinct, or in a stupor, or in superstitious illusion. The humanity of mankind merits further consideration. This is why I think that—here again, between faith and belief—we all share, in mourning others and ourselves, a *conduct* that exceeds knowledge, wisdom, and consciousness too.

A conduct that exceeds thinking, just as does another, symmetrical phenomenon, that of birth—these are the two sides of our fortuitousness—but whose excess precisely engages thought. Not only does our birth-death make us think, give us matter to think, but it truly opens thinking insofar as the latter is relation to the incommensurable, insofar as language constantly names the unnamable. In all its appearances, whether intellectual or artistic, practical or affective, thinking is sensibility to the unnamable: to what exceeds it and makes it possible. The unnamable is as terrible as it is dazzling, and its justice smacks of injustice. But it is definitively our drive—life- and death-drive, drive of desire and of pleasure. Drive of suffering and of *jouissance*. Thinking, language, affect: a thrusting that overflows itself. Sense, sensation, sentiment.

Between faith and belief, or more precisely, in the hollowing out of a triangle formed between faith, belief, and knowledge; in this hollowing out is suspended, undecided, trembling, a category that is not a true category, yet a real and consistent mode of feeling nonetheless: we should call it "belief without belief" or Freud's "disowning" (the translation of *Verleugnung*), but a disowning intertwined with an "as if." I know full well that there is no other world, but I believe, I want to believe, I allow the sketch of something possible, or rather not impossible, to form, of an unheard-of way of making sense, or not even sense but simply a way of conducting oneself and of caring for [*de se tenir et de tenir à*]—nothing, nothing but this desire or this nothing *as* this very desire to believe. Not an unhappy belief reduced to a pious wishing for itself, but the force of an impetus that does not take itself to be an imitation of knowledge but that opens within the impossible the possibility of relating to it. After all, is this not how we read literature and how it gives itself to be read? We believe in a tale [*récit*] that we know to be unreal and unbelievable. Thus we respond to the invitation of fiction, which proposes that we confect [*fictionner*], shape, figure (all the same concept) the unfigurable truth. But in fiction, truth is not figured as if by an impudent allegory: it is figured insofar as it is unfigurable. The infinite receives its finition, it opens within the finite.

And if the Adoration goes away, rings, his promise rings: "Away with these superstitions, these ancient bodies, these households and these ages. It is this epoch which has foundered!"

He will not go away, he will not redescend from a heaven, he will not accomplish the redemption of women's rages and of men's gaieties and all of this sin: for it is done, because of his being, and being loved."[29]

Appendix

Freud—So to Speak

1

Today we are being asked—the times demand it—to reassess what is at stake in Freud's intervention. We know more or less clearly that it did not arise from blending itself together with other bodies of recognized knowledge, nor did it add to them a new continent. Freud invented something other than knowledge—whether this is understood in the sense of a theoretical discipline or in that of a practical know-how. The very idea that practice (the clinic, as analysts say) should continue to bear responsibility for theory shows—even if at the risk of a certain pragmatist confusion—that here thinking proceeds from an opening to a thrust coming from depths that are ever more enigmatic, ever less available to "analysis," whatever meaning this word takes on. For the "clinic" consists in beating a path, each time in a singular way, toward this: that there is no access to any unveiling or primal sense. This is why Freud's invention is one of the most clearly and most resolutely non-religious of modern inventions. And also why it cannot believe in itself. It cannot avoid doing so insofar as it is an institution (not only the "schools," but also the simple analyst's practice, up to the disciplinary name of "psychoanalysis"), but as a way of thinking, its rule can only be to defer [*différer*] its own identity.

That analysis—and above all that of the "cure"—should be *interminable*, even when one declares it to be *finished* [terminée], is now clearly becoming an issue for what we call "Freudian psychoanalysis." It endlessly interprets itself or invites us to interpret it—and is therefore always getting further away from supposing itself to be a "knowledge" or "know-how." It is endlessly inviting us, beyond any analysis, to what Derrida calls a "lysis without measure, without measure and *without return*."[1]

In the final analysis—if you will—Freud is not looking for a knowledge. The evolution of his thinking demonstrates this: it endlessly displaces itself toward ever more expressly adventurous ("meta-psychological," which is to say, metaphysical or speculative) hypotheses or conjectures, toward less modelizable or constructible models ("second-topic," or rather a-topic), toward what Freud himself calls "speculation," "representation," or "myth" (the murder of the father, the death drive), and toward ever less clinical "objects"—such as religion, art, civilization, and war.

This is well known, but it merits reconsideration. We need more rigorously to take the measure of the gap that separates, for him, the positivity of the scientific and instrumental model (of which the "cure" is the main vehicle), on the one hand, from the narrative, imaginative, and creative thrust of a world on the other. For this is what Freud is looking for: to relate [*raconter*], to retrace the rise of being and the play of forces at work in it.

This does not mean that we should attempt to take the measure of this gap more accurately than has been done previously (for his part, Lacan was able to do so by inventing his own fiction of knowledge, which nonetheless remained under the instrumental imperatives of the institution and of its function, or of the profession).

2

What's more, what is at stake cannot be measured with a pair of compasses. Doubtless the gap of which we have been speaking grew throughout Freud's lifetime and thinking, but without reaching its full amplitude. But its essential motif or motive [*mobile*] runs all throughout his œuvre: the word *unconscious* does not designate a withdrawal of the soul, it is the soul itself, or, if you prefer, it is mankind. Freud does not discover mankind's unconscious in the way that Descartes thought he had discovered a pineal gland that had never previously been brought to light. Freud puts the whole human being into play. This is a new narrative [*récit*] of mankind.

It is the most resolutely non-religious narrative—which is to say, also the least disposed to give itself over to any sort of belief whatsoever, even a belief in science. Science's value for Freud is as a defense against religious illusion. But for him it does not have the reassuring qualities of an objective construction. It is only, at best, an index of firmness: namely, that we are not to give in to the illusions that attempt to transfigure us. As for the rest, Freud knows only too well that the desire for knowledge is part of the desire for power and mastery in general. Doubtless there is no "scholar" or "scientist" not only more modest than he but, above all, more sincerely open to uncertainties and to what is incomplete, even to the powerlessnesses of his knowledge.

Declarations of insufficiency, obscurity, or dissatisfaction pepper his œuvre. Whether he is discussing "identification," "sublimation," "art," or "civilization," among many other motifs, Freud demands that one accept the disappointment that his results create and that one proceed to other times and other resources. What he says about femininity, in concluding his paper on this topic, is valid in more than one way for the entirety of his work. Having admitted that his exposition is incomplete and fragmentary, he declares to his audience: "If you want to know more about it, enquire from your own experiences of life, turn to the poets, or wait until science can give you deeper and more coherent information."[2] Clearly, the last hypothesis is referring to a most uncertain future, if indeed it is not ironic, while the first two—which should be further linked to one another—clearly indicate, and in a way repeated many times in his œuvre, that this is a question less of knowing objects than of giving new expression to our existence as subjects.

3

Once we understand this situation, we can see that there is no Freudian "discovery," and the "unconscious" is not an organ. But there is undoubtably an invention: that of a narrative. Where man had been narrated as coming from a creator or from nature, where celestial life or survival as a species had been promised to him, Freud introduces a different provenance and destination. Man comes from an impetus or a thrust that surpasses it—that surpasses, in any case, what Freud designates as the "ego."

He calls this impetus or this thrust *Trieb*. In English, this is translated as *drive*. In French, the language in which I am writing, *pulsion* [pulsion] has been chosen.[3] Here the stakes of translation are particularly high. In two different ways, *drive* and *pulsion* put the accent on mechanical thrust, constraint. They are a traction that one undergoes rather than an attraction that one seeks. In French, the term *compulsion* accentuates this passive and almost automatic value of the movement that one undergoes, that is ordered from outside. But in Freud, compulsion is named *Zwang*, a word from a completely different family, referring to constraint, to the impossibility of resisting (particularly in the contexts of obsession and repetition). The two registers are quite distinct, even if they communicate at certain points.

In German, *Trieb* designates a thrust considered in its activity: the growth of a plant or the care that enables an animal to grow. It is of the order of impetus and desire. It carries itself forward, activates itself. A considerable, polymorphous activity is at work in the semantics of the verb *treiben*. Freud did not put this word forward by accident. He wants to hear in it at once more than an utterly programmed "instinct" and less than a programmatic "intention" or "aim." In truth, he hears in it a thrust that one undergoes—when seen through the eyes of the little, conscious, voluntary "me"—but that is also cooriginary with the birth and growth of this singular "one" that we name the "subject"—a term to which Freud gives little space—and that easily surpasses all that can be represented by our models of the "person" or of the "individual."

The *Trieb*—or the constellation of the *Triebe*—is a movement that comes from elsewhere, from the non-individuated, the buried, dispersed, proliferating, confused, archaic nature of our provenance—nature, the world, humanity behind us, and, behind it, all that makes it possible, the emergence of the sign and of the gesture, the call from one to the other and from all to the elements, the forces, the possible and the impossible, the sense of the infinite lying before, behind, and among us, the desire to respond to it and to expose ourselves to it. This movement, this impetus, this thrust, is our provenance; in the final analysis, it is in it and as it that we *thrust* [poussons], as we say in French of a plant: we rise up and become what we can be.

This thrust comes from elsewhere than from us. It makes us into a thrusted being, not a being "produced" by a network of causes, but dragged along, launched, projected, or even "thrown" (to take up Heidegger's word). This "elsewhere" is not, however, a beyond; it is not a transcendence, in the sense understood by theologies, nor is it a simple immanence, in the sense understood by those theologies that have been inverted into atheisms. This "elsewhere" is in us: it forms within us the most originary and the most energetic motor of the impetus that we are. For it is nothing less than our being, or rather, it is being itself as it proves to be, once detached from its ontological bindings. It is being as the verb *to be*: motion, movement, emotion, shaking, rising up of desire and of fear, awaiting [attente] and attempt, essay, outbreak [accès], crisis and exaltation, exasperation and exhaustion, formation of forms, invention of signs, uncontrollable tension up to the unbearable, where it breaks or rather settles out [*se dépose*].

4

What I am calling here Freud's "narrative" consists in this attempt to redraw mankind as the provenance and the coming of such a thrust: the growth of a sign traced out on an obscure background and infinitely opened to a being that no god, no nature, and no history can fill up with sense. It is the most powerful attempt that has been made since the end of the various metaphysics. It is able to escape the double trap of mankind's self-production, on the one hand (in which Marx, particularly, is caught), and, on the other, a resurrection of some kind of divinity (as in Heidegger's case).

This is also why its own greatness offers it to us suspended between dangers that threaten on either side: the positivity of a supposed science or technique (whose operatory properties cannot be denied, even if they are ever more visibly limited by the deep mutation of civilization and with it that of the "psyche"), and the belief in who knows what depths or phantasmatic powers, the entire imaginary of a "primitivity" that psychoanalysis consists precisely in calling into question.

But what it calls into question, whether as a supposed object or as a fabulous origin, is nothing less than its own consistency: this is what underpins what we are naming here the Freudian narrative. This narrative relates that—and how—mankind relates its provenance to itself in relation to an infinite surpassing of itself, to an excessive thrust that precedes and follows it, that sets it in the world and removes it from the world, even as this thrust demands that it give form in this world to this otherworldly force.

In *Mass Psychology and Analysis of the Ego*, Freud sets on stage the first storyteller [*récitant*], the first mythologian, who recounts to his tribe that he has killed the father: a tale of the impossible, since the father only comes about through the murder, in which one therefore will only ever have killed the prepaternal animal. Here Freud writes that myth is what allows the individual to escape mass psychology. In other words, myth is what allows the structure according to which an "ego" can detach itself from the backdrop of the "id" in order to appear—and this detachment takes place via the mythical production of the "hero," which is to say, of "me." Freud's whole invention opens up here: the subject recounts himself, he comes about through his narrative. This is no tall tale [*fabulation*], as the "speaking subject" is not operating here, it is rather he who is placed in the world by word—word, or what could better be named significance, the opening of a possibility of sense.

Freud knew that one must not demand sense (or the meaning of life) [*demander le sens (de la vie)*]; he says that this demand is already pathological. But he knew that significance obliges us. To be obliged by sense is to have to posit oneself as being carried off by what one has the task of carrying. This is what speech as myth responds to: it does not tell tall tales, it does not confect [*fictionne*], it attempts to allow to speak what precedes speech, namely, significance in its perpetually nascent state. *Trieb*—thrust, impetus, beating, enthusiasm, fit of anger—is the name that Freud finds (expressly against "instinct") to put into words this effort, this forcing of sense from before and after all signification: the force of a desire that carries mankind well beyond itself.

To the precise point where science stops and religion proves to be an illusion, where Freud reopens the mythical word. Where he gives a name, which is provisional, as are all mythical names (and perhaps therefore all names . . .), to what thrusts in being. Was he not able to write: "The theory of the drives is, so to speak, our mythology. Drives are mythical entities, magnificent in their indefiniteness"?[4]

"So to speak" (*sozusagen*): but one always speaks "so," by approximation, more or less, as closely as possible to and always infinitely far away from what will have driven us to speak.[5]

Notes

Prologue

1. [Nancy quotes from Ludwig Wittgenstein, *Remarques sur 'Le Rameau d'or' de Frazer*, trans. Jean Lacoste and Jacques Bouveresse (Geneva: L'âge d'homme, 1982), 25. Strangely, this passage is absent from the bilingual edition, *Bermerkungen uber Frazers 'Golden Bough'/Remarks on Frazer's 'Golden Bough,'* ed. Rush Rees, trans. A. C. Miles (Atlantic Highlands. N.J.: Humanities, 1993).—Trans.]

1. There Is No Sense of Sense: That Is Worthy of Adoration

1. [Nancy quotes Hölderlin, *Antigone de Sophocle*, trans. Philippe Lacoue-Labarthe (Paris: Bourgois, 1978), 49. Given the idiosyncrasy of Hölderlin's translation and the importance of Lacoue-Labarthe for Nancy's thought, I have chosen to translate the passage quoted, rather than to use an existing English translation of Sophocles.—Trans.]

2. Ernesto Sabato, *El Tunel* (Barcelona: Seix Barral, 1983), 42–43 [my translation—Trans.].

3. William Faulkner, *The Sound and the Fury* (New York: Cape and Smith, 1929), 152.

4. Nonetheless, there is much here that could be retained: for example, in Augustine or in Eckhart, affirming that God is constantly creating the world (his "eternity" not being a time before time but the creation of time, outside time itself); or, of course, in Isaac Luria and his famous thought of the withdrawal [*retrait*] of God as a creator (*tsim-tsoum*); or even in possible commentaries on the Qu'ran's affirmation of God, according to which he has no problem in recommencing indefinitely (30, 27), among others.

5. On the "void" used as a name for "the properties of physical space expunged of real particles" and at the same time for a "minimal state of energy within a field," see Michel Cassé, *Du vide et de la création* (Paris: Odile Jacob, 1995).

6. Immanuel Kant, "Religion Within the Boundaries of Mere Reason," 4th part, 2nd section, "General Remark," in *Religion and Rational Theology*, trans. and ed. Allen W. Wood and George di Giovanni (Cambridge: Cambridge University Press, 1996), 212 (emphasis original).

7. The Christian "sermon" is the part of the service reserved, at the margin of the cult, for ordinary discourse.

8. Nearly a quotation of the last page of Derrida's *On Touching—Jean-Luc Nancy*, trans. Christine Irizarry (Stanford, Calif.: Stanford University Press, 2005).

9. I have had occasion to speak of "transimmanence": the semantic combination is clear, but the underlying thinking remains labored, lacking the intuitive form for the linguistic sentiment.

10. Sura, 61, 55.

2. In the Midst of the World

NOTE: [A version of this chapter is included in *Re-treating Religion: Deconstructing Christianity with Jean-Luc Nancy*, ed. Alena Alexandrova, Ignaas Devisch, Laurens Ten Kate, and Aukje van Rooden (New York: Fordham University Press, 2011), 1–21.—Trans.]

EPIGRAPH: Paul Celan, "Mandorla," in *Poems of Paul Celan*, trans. Michael Hamburger (London: Anvil Press Poetry, 1995), 192. As a technical term in art history, *mandorla* designates the elliptical, almondlike shape inside which Christ in Majesty is depicted; this motif often appears above the great doors of a church, in miniatures, in stained-glass windows, etc.

1. That Christianity should be as Greek as it is Jewish—and as Jewish as it is Greek, Joyce would have said—is what we learn from historians such as Moses Finley or Arnaldo Momigliano. In general terms, the deployment of Christianity disguised the complexity of its provenance, when in fact this provenance allows us to understand how this deployment was a response to a profound movement in the Mediterranean world. On this topic, see Paul Veyne, *Quand notre monde est devenu chrétien (312–394)* (Paris: Albin Michel, 2007). A more provocative work was recently published by Bruno Delorme, *Le Christ grec: De la tragédie aux Evangiles* (Paris: Bayard, 2009).

2. It is not a question of merely contributing a certain representation: at issue is a mutation of affect and of existential dispositions. As Günther Anders states quite rightly, "each foundation of a religion [is] a veritable revolution in the emotional history of humanity, a veritable refoundation of sentiment." See *L'obsolescence de l'homme* (Paris: Ivrea, 2002), 347. This remark is important because it displaces the most common characterization of religions as systems of representation (fantastical or not). Their representational schemes are in effect nothing

other than the taking shape of a nascent sentiment as it attempts to express itself. When a civilization has defined itself as being outside or beyond religion, it calls in turn for a new sensibility, and that is indeed what Anders set out to communicate in this book from 1956. Without following in his footsteps, we can, like him, recognize that the "melancholy of the nihilist" is indeed the affect that arouses in us protest and the desire for revolution.

3. Ludwig Wittgenstein, *Tractatus Logico-Philosophicus*, trans. D. F. Pears and B. F. McGuiness (New York: Humanities, 1961), 6.41, p. 145.

4. Peter Brown, *The Body and Society: Men, Women and Sexual Renunciation in Early Christianity* (New York: Columbia University Press, 1988), 186–87.

5. See, e.g., his *Critique of Practical Reason*, pt. 1, bk. 1, chap. 3: "Of the Motives [*Triebfedern*] of Pure Practical Reason."

6. In the period of Christianity's first growth, it also had strong recourse to the opposition between worlds or realms, which was expressed in the "gnoses" where Christianity and Manicheism mingled. The gnostic temptation, which reappears periodically in new forms and can be seen to innervate puritanisms and the religiosity of "sects," bears witness to a double desire: at once to sharpen the opposition between one realm and the other, between light and darkness, and to appropriate a knowledge (the meaning of "gnosis") of this opposition. This temptation thus signals precisely what it is important to move away from.

7. See Jacques Derrida, *On Touching—Jean-Luc Nancy*, trans. Christine Irizarry (Stanford, Calif.: Stanford University Press, 2005). [In French *salut* can mean both "greeting or salutation" and "salvation."—Trans.]

8. The claim that Socrates and Christ can be identified with one another confronts head-on the opposition that is usually established between the two, most elaborately by Kierkegaard. Indeed, for him the truth discovered by recollection is incompatible with the truth for which a subject must break off and be reborn. I do not wish to oppose this thesis, no more than to subscribe to it: I wish to consider a structural similarity where the "right here" of the "outside" essentially passes to one side of the contrast underlined by Kierkegaard. But what is at stake is still the same "passion of the infinite" (Søren Kierkegaard, *Concluding Unscientific Postscript* [Princeton: Princeton University Press, 1968], 192).

9. [*Déposition* has several meanings: (1) deposing an authority figure; (2) an account given under oath, a submission; (3) the representation of the body of Jesus as it is being taken down from the cross; (4) to deposit something, such as a thesis in a library.—Trans.]

10. Claude Lévi-Strauss, *The Naked Man: Mythologiques 4*, trans. John and Doreen Weightman (Chicago: University of Chicago Press, 1990), 694, trans. modified.

11. ["Christianity" is *christianisme* in French. *Chrétienté* has been translated as "Christendom" throughout.—Trans.]

12. Heidegger shows this in *The Principle of Reason*, trans. Reginald Lilly (Bloomington: Indiana University Press, 1991).

13. For Jan Assmann, nothing less than "the original impulse of biblical monotheism" is to be found "in its capacity to trace a boundary between domination and salvation, between political power and divine power, and to dispossess the leaders of the world of salvation and religious leaders of violence" (*Violence et monothéisme*, trans. J. Schmutz [Paris: Bayard, 2009], 10. See also Assmann's "Wiener Vorlesung" of 2006, *Monotheismus und die Sprache der Gewalt* [Vienna: Picus, 2006]). I refer the reader to Assmann for the background to this thesis, to which I think that (Judeo-)Christianity and Islam give two different, even divergent, developments, though both are indeed developments of this "tracing of boundaries," despite all the contrary indications to be found in the history of these religions. Among the historical characteristics that one could gather to show that the distinction between the "powers" of this world and of heaven plays a cardinal role throughout Christianity, I choose this one: the university, when it appeared in the high Middle Ages, was qualified as the "third power." This shows that it responded to the conception of autonomous knowledge as an activity independent of the two powers that were exercised as spiritual power and political power—both outside of knowledge, of the idea of free knowledge.

14. Dostoevsky's Prince Myshkin encapsulates this auto-apostasy: "In my opinion, Roman Catholicism is not even a faith, it's a continuation of the Western Roman Empire, and everything in it is subordinated to that idea, beginning with their faith. The pope seized the earth, an earthly throne, and took up the sword; since that time everything has gone the same way, except that to the sword they've added lies, intrigue, deceit, fanaticism, superstition, and evil-doing. They have trifled with the most sacred, truthful, innocent, and ardent emotions of the people and bartered them all, all of them, for money and paltry temporal power. Is not this the teaching of Antichrist? Atheism was bound to come from them! Atheism did come from them, from Roman Catholicism itself! Atheism first came into being through them: could they believe in themselves?" (Fyodor Dostoevsky, *The Idiot* [Oxford: Oxford University Press, 1992], 574). One must, of course, also consider the "continuation" of the Eastern Roman Empire. There is much to be said about the relations of the Orthodox Churches to "paltry temporal power." But this is not the place to do so, no more than to examine the role of the Reformation in the evolution of the relations between Churches and States. In one sense, and from the perspective adopted here, the Roman Church sets the tone for our consideration of the inner contradiction between the separation and the distinction of the "kingdoms." But there is no reason to be content with condemning this Church alone or more than others: it is rather a reason to ask oneself what, with the collapse of Rome and the possibility of a "civil religion," caused the West to enter into this contradiction, in which Islam was perhaps formed from the beginning, but which it was long able to resolve in its own way. *What dissociated men from their gods, what made it so that "myth," on the one hand, and "idol," on the other, became the names of illusion and dishonesty—that is the event in which we find our origin.* An irreversible, enduring event, from which we are not yet able to take our leave.

15. What's more, this hatred is deployed in the epoch when the Roman Church is engaged in the Crusades, which is to say, in the enterprise most obviously contradictory to the separation of the "kingdoms."

16. The Church's forging of the expression "deicidal people" (which it eventually abandoned) is theologically so incoherent that the hatred behind it becomes glaringly obvious: if God had to die for the salvation of mankind, then deicide or deicides clearly entered into the economy of this salvation. This is a point that has been commented upon, just as the role or sense of Judas in the history of Jesus' passion has been abundantly commented upon and discussed.

17. Of course, one ought to be much more precise with regard to this history. In the feudal epoch, even if feudalism is implicated both in the monarchies and in the first attempts at establishing a new Western Empire, there is something that can—or must—be distinguished from the simultaneity (conflictual or not) of the two realms or the two swords. There is a stronger mutual intrication between the religious order and the order of vassalage and suzerainty, where the values of the oath of allegiance and of fidelity—and thus of a sworn faith—play a major role. The particularity of this formation only brings out more clearly the difference between it and the modern or premodern state that succeeds it and makes the separation between the orders much more stark. The sovereignty of the state is not suzerainty. The latter operates, one could say, according to a religious politics [*politique*]; the former clears religion away. Eventually, sovereignty of the state tends towards a "civil religion," which it fails to institute because the state's essence is not religious and because at bottom it is entirely "of this world." One might think that today Islam is opening in Europe the possibility that this distinction might be set to work in a wholly new way.

18. At the most I could mention, in accordance with the what has been said by thinkers and historians who are competent in these matters, that the caliphate was instituted via modalities that did not truly originate in the sayings and writings of the Prophet, and to which the clashes between tribes after Mohammed's death were not unconnected. Nonetheless, the sentiment of the necessary distinction has not failed to appear in the history of Islam (e.g., when Ibn Arabi distinguishes prophets, sheiks, and sovereigns).

19. Here I intersect—albeit in a rather different spirit—with the thinking of Whitehead, who speaks of "the present immediacy of a kingdom not of this world"; see the chapter "God and the World" in *Process and Reality* (New York: Free Press, 1978), 343.

20. Serge Margel, *Le silence des prophètes: La falsification des Écritures et le destin de la modernité* (Paris: Galilée, 2006), 265.

21. Not "indiscernible" in the sense that Leibniz gives it, that is, where two realities cannot be brought back to the same essence, of which they would simply be multiple realizations. That is to say, also in the sense where an existence must be considered to be an "individual essence." There is certainly much to explore in examining the question of singularity within the order of technical objects and of existence insofar as it is caught up in technical relations. To find and to open

the order of the singular in the apparent indiscernibility of the technical order is one of our tasks.

22. In truth, philosophy and literature share this function, in a sharing that is extremely complex and always in transformation. This is beyond the scope of the present chapter.

23. J. M. Coetzee, *Elizabeth Costello* (London: Vintage, 2004), 150. [Nancy quotes from the French translation by Catherine Lauga du Plessis (Paris: Seuil, 2004), which uses *adoration* for "worship."—Trans.]

3. Mysteries and Virtues

1. *Nietzsche Werke: Kritische Gesamtausgabe*, vol. 7.3, *Nachgelassene Fragmente: Herbst 1884 bis Herbst 1885* (Berlin: de Gruyter, 1974), 206.

2. More precisely, if the last step of an initiation was that of the *epopt*, the initiate who opens her eyes and contemplates the "mysterious" secret (the phallus, *fascinus*, face of Isis, theophany), the initiation itself was the doing of the *mystes*, a term whose primary meaning is closure—of the mouth or eyes. The word prevailed in a tradition that, from the letters of Paul onward, gave it the sense of "revealed truth" (*apocalypsis mysteriou*, Romans 16:25)—from Neoplatonism onward, it received the values that we associate with "mystical." But even before that, the *mystes* is already the one who, proceeding in the initiation, penetrates into the secret and who therefore "opens" her eyes (or mouth) in the very gesture of closing them. This is another sort of vision or speech. On the one hand, Christian usage retains something of this value—which belongs to the three monotheisms as the value of "revelation." On the other hand, no element of a reserved initiation, that which is secret in itself, has been retained. At this initial stage, the conclusion is already that the gaze opens itself to a vision of the outside, speech speaks in an adoration that goes beyond words.

3. The Apocalypse of John leads one astray if one sees its figures of solar illumination, flaming apparitions, gleaming gold, and precious stones as a paradigm of "revelation" or of "unveiling" (this is the sense of the former word). One should not forget that all this grand spectacle also leads to "a new heaven and a new earth" that need neither sun, moon, nor lights (chapter 21). Theirs is a different light.

In *Survivance des lucioles* (Paris: Minuit, 2009), which I am reading as I complete this book, Georges Didi-Huberman contrasts light [*luce*] and firefly [*lucciole*] in a way that has resonances for me. In a singular coincidence, he does this in terms of Pasolini, whom I quote below. This common reference is not unconnected to what Didi-Huberman names "a community of desire, a community of lights emitted" (133), which for him prevents any reconstitution of the overbearing and blinding light of a "metaphysical cosmos" or "theological dogma" (75).

4. Pier Paolo Pasolini, *Actes impurs*, trans. R. de Ceccatty (Paris: Gallimard, 1983), 111.

5. Let the issue of machismo not be raised here. With or without Freud, we know that virility is no more the reserve of boys than tenderness is that of girls.

6. See the Appendix below, "Freud—So to Speak."

7. One cannot be content to speak, as is often the case, of a spiritual "progress" of Mediterranean humanity: there is no "progress"; there is a mutation with anthropological consequences. That Buddhism—also often presented as "spiritual progress"—should be more or less contemporary with this mutation is a remarkable phenomenon, which I do not have the means to explore.

8. I shall not enter into the discussion that long ago led to the great schism between Eastern and Western Christianity. It was mainly motivated by the question of precedence between spirit and son, but for us the very object of the debate disappears: there is no precedence where a strict simultaneity is in play. The relation is given at the same time as its terms, which do not exist without it.

9. Jacques Derrida, *On Touching—Jean-Luc Nancy*, trans. Christine Irizarry (Stanford, Calif.: Stanford University Press, 2005), 310 (trans. modified): "And let it be—blessed, like a still unthinkable benediction, an exasperated benediction, a benediction *accorded*, and accorded to his 'exasperated consent' and in accordance with it, a benediction without any hope of salvation or salute, an ex-hoped-for/exasperated [*exespéré*] *salut*, an incalculable salutation or one without calculation, an unpresentable salutation, renouncing Salvation in advance, as should any salute worthy of the name.// *Salut* without salvation; a just *salut* just to come." (The words Derrida puts in quotation marks are from Nancy.)

10. Not all languages have a word derived from the idea of the unharmed [*sauf*] or the saved [*sauvé*] with which salutations are made. But all languages are able to salute. However one might translate "salut!" its exclamation mark will remain out of harm's way [*sauf*]. . . Perhaps we should say that in all languages the word addressed also addresses a greeting [*salut*], even in the absence of a special formulation.

11. What does the tale of "original sin" tell us? That we must not touch a certain fruit in the divine garden. To touch is to attempt to grasp what is given and must remain given, must be received as a gift, not appropriated. The sin comes down to grasping the gift, to incorporating it by knowledge and by absorption. Forgiving sin allows this grasping to let go. Grasping [*se saisir de*]/letting go [*se dessaisir de*]. . . : this beating rhythms us.

12. I shall say no more here about Christian grace, apart from noting this: except in its extreme versions, where it becomes the arbitrary power of an inexorable God (which is to say, of a cruel consciousness), grace has more value through being received and accepted than through being granted. That it is granted means that all virtue and all salvation come from elsewhere, from outside, and return there. Virtue is always also the exercise of a welcome extended to grace.

13. See Matthew 21:31–21.

14. Friedrich Nietzsche, *Thus Spake Zarathustra*, trans. Thomas Common (Mineola: Dover Thrift, 1999), "The Convalescent," 2, 153–54 (trans. modified). The verb that Nietzsche uses—*grüssen*—means "to salute" and has no relation with "to save." Its provenance concerns the addressed word; the English word *to greet* comes from the same root.

15. Here I need not quote the well-known verses of Paul in his first Letter to the Corinthians.

16. It is less well known, less visible, and yet definitely significant that philosophy refuses or disdains riches, particularly what can be earned by teaching the *logos*, just as it rejects unlegitimated power, the reign of the strongest. The figure of the *sophist* is the emblem of both, a bête noire that philosophy partly discovers and partly creates. This is a way of demonstrating doubly that a relation that is somehow pure, lacking any given observance, demands that its own laws be found. But doubtless here as elsewhere the law can never suffice, nor can any sort of calculus, knowledge, or measure. If Plato "prepared the way for Christianity," as Pascal thinks, that is in opening toward passing beyond any kind of legitimacy, when it comes to how relation must exist, that could be verified, guaranteed, or known. ("Opening" here means both "despite himself" and "in his own movement." Both postulations can be found in Plato. In general terms, philosophy will have constantly been opening in this way, as if by conjoined excess and default, onto a passing beyond of its own reason: onto a dis-enclosure.)

17. Of course, we must not falsify our vision of an order in which the shimmering of glory was far from being pure and which knew the spirit of lucre together with the downtrodden poor. Nonetheless, possibilities for investment, profit, and "growth" had not been invented, or at least deployed. To simplify, we can say that hoarding (inert accumulation) was prevalent and that capitalization (active accumulation) came to replace it. Riches became suspect or an object of infamy in a world passing from the former to the latter. Much later, Christianity will be provoked by the accusation of hoarding (with the Franciscans, then the Reformation) to privilege active accumulation—meant to be favorable to the common good. Capitalism, democracy, and the deconstruction of Christianity came about together, at once each thanks to the other, each in the other, and each despite the other. We must learn to free ourselves from this assemblage and never return to it, without going back to hoarding either, or to hierarchy, or to Christianity.

18. This is the invention of the "individual" or "subject" and, with it, of a separation and a solitude unknown to other cultures. While it will take a long time before becoming itself as we recognize it, or think we do, this is already the subjectivity that comes about with Christianity, or rather "as" Christianity, after passing through various preliminary philosophical stages, particularly in stoicism. Christianity nonetheless represents the movement of a "subject" that finds or identifies itself only in losing itself in an infinite opening of itself. This is the main burden of Augustine's "interior intimo meo, superior summo meo." This "more interior than my intimacy, more elevated than my summit" is nothing other than God. But this also means that "God," if he "is," is nothing other than this infinite excess of "me" over myself, my "ek-sistence" itself, as Heidegger writes, which is inseparable from my relation to another to whom I am exposed and open. This other is not another individual but is, in each subject and between all of us, we beings, this same excess turned around and stretched toward the

outside of the world that opens up in the midst of the world. In order to be precise, we should no doubt say that the individual does not appear alone but is accompanied (even preceded?) by the "person," which is to say, by the legal and moral subject. Modern reason has tried to accentuate the person by imputing to it both responsibility and existential dignity. But it has not been able to open (should one say sufficiently?) the person either to the excess in question or to a dimension beyond the individual (let us say a "common" dimension, if not a "communitarian" one, while thinking that "communism" carried this demand without recognizing it). According to Levinas, "responsibility" alone provides an exception to the limitation of the person and the individual, and in a way that well and truly opens onto an outside that is right here. However, the difference in perspectives calls for a whole other analysis.

19. See Sigmund Freud, *Civilization and Its Discontents*, parts 5 and 8.

20. The Greek of the *koinē* used *agapeō* as a polite salutation, just as the Romans used *carus*, and as we do in saying "my dear," "dear Sir . . .," or even "dearest" [*chéri*]. It is as if the lexicons of civility, love, and faith had taken up the idea of "price" at the moment when riches were leaving the age of glory and entering the first age of enrichment. A banalization and devaluation of all values were therefore produced in what Marx would subsume under a "general equivalence." Charity attempts to make us consider an equivalence or equality in absolute distinction, and therefore in the thoroughgoing non-equivalence of the objects that this distinction loves piously.

21. There is one well-known objection: the question of whether one should love criminals and the mentally defective. This objection confuses a desiring or tender love with just love, which involves considerations of incommensurable dignity, a dignity incommensurable even to the "person" himself. This is ultimately what opposition to the death penalty rests upon.

22. Emmanuel Levinas, *Outside the Subject*, trans. Michael B. Smith (London: Athlone, 1994), 28.

23. Søren Kierkegaard, *Works of Love*, ed. and trans. Howard V. Hong and Edna H. Hong (Princeton: Princeton University Press, 1995), 66. For Kierkegaard, this love is opposed to the predilection of the love of a singular person. He nonetheless brings the two together in a single quality of "blinding," which ultimately represents the impossibility of giving reasons [*rendre raison*]. I shall come back elsewhere to the connection and disparity in the "without reason" of the equality of all and of the exclusivity of passion, of "human rights" and of "the fury of the senses," of justice and possession.

24. This force is declared by *amen* or *amîn*, which Christians and Muslims have retained from the Jewish tradition.

25. Jacques Derrida, "Faith and Knowledge: The Two Sources of 'Religion' at the Limits of Reason Alone," trans. Samuel Weber, in *Acts of Religion*, ed. Gil Anidjar (New York: Routledge, 2002), 96.

26. William Faulkner, *Requiem for a Nun* (New York: Random House, 1951), 281 (thanks to Jean-Pierre Daumard).

27. Ibn Khaldun, *Le livre des exemples*, trans. A. Cheddadi (Paris: Gallimard, 2002), 6, 30.

28. *Nietzsche Werke: Kritische Gesamtausgabe*, vol. 8.1, *Nachgelassene Fragmente: Herbst 1885 bis Herbst 1887* (Berlin: de Gruyter, 1974), 287.

29. See Jean-Luc Nancy, *The Truth of Democracy*, trans. Pascale-Anne Brault and Michel Naas (New York: Fordham University Press, 2010), and "Finite and Infinite Democracy," in *Democracy in What State?* trans. William McCuaig (New York: Columbia University Press, 2011), 58–75.

4. Complements, Supplements, Fragments

1. J. M. Coetzee, *Elizabeth Costello: Eight Lessons* (London: Vintage, 2004), 188.

2. See Jean-Luc Nancy, *Le plaisir du dessin* (Paris: Galilée, 2009), which unfolds this logic. [Forthcoming from Fordham University Press as *The Pleasure in Drawing*, trans. Philip Armstrong.—Trans.]

3. Baruch Spinoza, *Ethics*, trans. W. H. White, rev. A. H. Stirling (Ware: Wordsworth, 2001), 255.

4. Qu'ran, 17, 23. One can note the discussion of "to adore" as a translation introduced by Youssef Seddick in *Le Coran—autre lecture, autre tradition* (Algiers, Barzakh/La Tour d'Aigues: L'Aube, 2002), 140.

5. Ibn Arabi, *Traité de l'amour*, trans. M. Gloton (Paris: Albin Michel, 1986), 227.

6. *Les dits de Bastami*, trans. A. Meddeb (Paris: Fayard, 1989), 90.

7. Franz Kafka, *Journal*, trans. Marthe Robert (Paris: Grasset, 1954).

8. Nicole Debrand, "L'enquête," *Po&sie*, 127 (Paris: Belin, 2009).

9. Angel Vazquez, *La chienne de vie de Juanita Narboni* (Lyon: Rouge Inside, 2009), 85 (thanks to Hélène).

10. Jacques Derrida, *Of Spirit: Heidegger and the Question*, trans. Geoffrey Bennington and Rachel Bowlby (Chicago: University of Chicago Press, 1989), 107 (italics original).

11. Heraclitus, fragment B51 of the Diels-Kranz as Hölderlin transposed it, a transposition that made the formulation famous in the form quoted here.

12. In the initial Latin version of the text, Descartes wrote "ego sum," a formulation in which the pronoun is not prescribed, as it is in French, since the verbal form already indicates it; Descartes is therefore trying to underline the gap, the difference from themselves of both "ego" and "sum."

13. This sentence is in the present tense, because we should not think that reproduction is entirely behind us. There is always an element of it at the heart of production, in the same way that the latter began before its schema became dominant.

14. It is no accident that the thinking of Locke, then that of Rousseau and Marx, turn so importantly around property and appropriation. Marx attempts to indicate, at the extreme point of his thinking, an "individual property" that would be neither private nor collective, which we should doubtless understand,

beyond and through the property of goods, as a property whereby the "individual"—here understood as a person in the bosom of a community—would appropriate his own true being.

15. John Maynard Keynes, "Economic Possibilities for Our Grandchildren," in *Essays in Persuasion* (London: Macmillan and Co., 1931), 372. Thanks to Frédéric Postel.

16. Martin Heidegger, "Letter on Humanism," in *Basic Writings*, ed. David Farrell Krell (London: Routledge, 1977), 213–65.

17. *Gestell*, Heidegger's word, which can be translated and glossed as armor, structure, and installation, as the entirely constructed, consistent, and opaque character of a world built on the exhaustion of nature and the turning away of the gods.

18. Some will undoubtedly think here of a certain salutation, the German *Heil!*, which has the same meaning as "unharmed" [*sauf*] and which the Nazis degraded. It is necessary to separate the salutation addressed to idols from that addressed from one to another.

19. By saying *cela* and *ça* I am nodding toward Freud, but allusively. [The French translation of "id" is *ça*.—Trans.] The disposition of "id" and "ego" [*moi*] should be reconfigured quite differently, and perhaps we should leave behind us the "id" of the vaguely inferior and obscure state of a magma in which we imagine it to lie. Because "id" is the world itself. As for the "superego," I have the same reservations about it as I do about politics, religion, and even art when they refer to an instituted, configured regime. One could say: adoration springs forth from the id, transfixes the ego, and returns to the id. That is sense.

20. The first version of this passage was written for a day of homage to Roland Barthes organized by Julia Kristeva in 2009, whose proceedings are to be published.

21. See Ludwig Wittgenstein, *Tractatus Logico-Philosophicus*, trans. D. F. Pears and B. F. McGuiness (New York: Humanities, 1961), 6.41, p. 145. Cf. 6.4312: "The solution of the riddle of life in space and time lies *outside* space and time"; and the consequence (6.432), "*How* the world is, is completely indifferent for what is higher. God does not reveal himself *in* the world." This needs to be corrected or made more specific (according to what Wittgenstein's last intention is imagined to have been) as follows: in the world an outside is revealed that has no other place than the very opening of the inside.

22. I shall not elaborate on this here, having done so in various texts, particularly *The Truth of Democracy*, trans. Pascale-Anne Brault and Michel Naas (New York: Fordham University Press, 2010), and "Finite and Infinite Democracy," in *Democracy in What State?* trans. William McCuaig (New York: Columbia University Press, 2011), 58–75.

23. While I was working on this book, Hugo Santiago wrote to me that if one speaks of faith, one has to speak of what lies beyond death, that that is the touchstone of "faith." What would I say to this? I responded to him, then after I had transformed the letter into a part of this text, it seemed more just to keep—with

H. S.'s agreement—the letter as it was: doubtless it gives a better idea of the inevitable trembling of thinking. I have added only the last two paragraphs and the footnotes.

24. [Nancy italicizes the article of *le mort* in order to bring out the distinction from *la mort*, death. The gesture is repeated later on in the letter.—Trans.]

25. Jean-Luc Nancy, *Noli me tangere: On the Raising of the Body*, trans. Sarah Clift, Pascale-Anne Brault, and Michael Naas (New York: Fordham University Press, 2008).

26. This phrase concludes the few lines that Jacques Derrida had written to be read by his oldest son at his burial, at which Hugo Santiago was present. They were addressed to all those who were present and of course beyond that, to everyone. Some treacherous minds have attempted to read them as a religious statement: this is to be incapable of deciphering "wherever I might be" [*où que je sois*]. See "Final Words," trans. Gila Walker, in *The Late Derrida*, ed. W. J. T. Mitchell and Arnold I. Davidson (Chicago: University of Chicago Press, 2007), 244 (trans. modified).

27. [Nancy writes "'concevoir les choses sous une espèce d'identité' (pour prendre la traduction de Pautrat)."—Trans.]

28. According to various cultures, this conduct takes one of three fundamental appearances: either haunting (the dead survive by constantly haunting the living, who must reconcile them); or the sojourn of shadows (the dead lead a sort of inferior life, pale and drab); or eternal life/death—the dead bear the truth of their life and of life itself, a truth that can be translated as "glorious body," as an annihilated body (two Western versions), or as a metempsychic body (an Oriental version). This conduct is never free from dread, just as it is never without trust: it always affirms in one way or another that life passes [*passe*] death. But "to survive" cannot therefore be resolved dialectically or as a religious consolation. But "passing," "passing away" [*trépasser*], makes a sign that is irreducible to any solution, to any salvation, as it is to any dissolution and to any purely scandalous affirmation (as one often says). The "conduct" I am discussing is that whereby men receive this sign without understanding it—and yet comprehending that this sign comprehends them. A sign or a stigma [*stigme*] that divides [*partage*] heaven and earth, day and night, infinite and finite, absence and presence, the beyond and the here: that divides and shares us all between one another and in ourselves, and that, in dividing and sharing the world, makes it a world.

29. Arthur Rimbaud, from "Genius," no. 40 in "The Illuminations," in *A Season in Hell* and *The Illuminations*, trans. Enid Rhodes Peschel (New York: Oxford University Press, 1973), 171–73.

Appendix: Freud—So to Speak

NOTE: Originally published in French in *Po&sie* 124 (Paris: Belin, 2008).

1. Jacques Derrida, *Resistances of Psychoanalysis*, trans. Peggy Kamuf, Pascale-Anne Brault, and Michael Naas (Stanford, Calif.: Stanford University Press, 1998), 34 (emphasis original).

2. Sigmund Freud, "Femininity," in *The Standard Edition of the Complete Psychological Works*, ed. and trans. James Strachey, vol. 22, *New Introductory Lectures on Psycho-Analysis and Other Works* (London: Hogarth Press and the Institute of Psychoanalysis, 1964), 135.

3. [In the rest of the book, *pulsion* has been translated as "drive," an option obviously inappropriate here.—Trans.]

4. Sigmund Freud, "Anxiety and Instinctual Life," in *The Standard Edition of the Complete Psychological Works*, ed. and trans. James Strachey, vol. 22, *New Introductory Lectures on Psycho-Analysis and Other Works*, 95, translation modified.

5. Wittgenstein said, in an interview on Freud: "He did not explain a myth scientifically. Rather, he forged a new myth. The affirmation that all anxiety is a repetition of the anxiety of the trauma of birth, for example, attracts us in precisely the way that a mythology does. 'Everything stems from something much further back.' Almost like the relation to the dead" (*Vorlesungen und Gespräche über Ästhetik, Psychoanalyse une religiösen Glauben* [Frankfurt a. M.: Fischer, 2000], 73, originally translated into German by Ralf Funke and retranslated into English here from Nancy's French version). Even if this remark has a critical tone, it does show that Wittgenstein, who, by the way, was evidently unaware of the text on drives as "mythical beings," clearly perceives Freud's sensibility to an infinitely withdrawn anteriority.

Perspectives in
Continental Philosophy

John D. Caputo, series editor

Karl Jaspers, *The Question of German Guilt*. Introduction by Joseph W. Koterski, S.J.

Jean-Luc Marion, *The Idol and Distance: Five Studies*. Translated with an introduction by Thomas A. Carlson.

Jeffrey Dudiak, *The Intrigue of Ethics: A Reading of the Idea of Discourse in the Thought of Emmanuel Levinas*.

Robyn Horner, *Rethinking God as Gift: Marion, Derrida, and the Limits of Phenomenology*.

Mark Dooley, *The Politics of Exodus: Søren Kierkegaard's Ethics of Responsibility*.

Merold Westphal, *Overcoming Onto-Theology: Toward a Postmodern Christian Faith*.

Edith Wyschogrod, Jean-Joseph Goux, and Eric Boynton, eds., *The Enigma of Gift and Sacrifice*.

Stanislas Breton, *The Word and the Cross*. Translated with an introduction by Jacquelyn Porter.

Jean-Luc Marion, *Prolegomena to Charity*. Translated by Stephen E. Lewis.

Peter H. Spader, *Scheler's Ethical Personalism: Its Logic, Development, and Promise*.

Jean-Louis Chrétien, *The Unforgettable and the Unhoped For*. Translated by Jeffrey Bloechl.

Don Cupitt, *Is Nothing Sacred? The Non-Realist Philosophy of Religion: Selected Essays*.

Jean-Luc Marion, *In Excess: Studies of Saturated Phenomena*. Translated by Robyn Horner and Vincent Berraud.

Phillip Goodchild, *Rethinking Philosophy of Religion: Approaches from Continental Philosophy*.

William J. Richardson, S.J., *Heidegger: Through Phenomenology to Thought*.

Jeffrey Andrew Barash, *Martin Heidegger and the Problem of Historical Meaning*.

Jean-Louis Chrétien, *Hand to Hand: Listening to the Work of Art*. Translated by Stephen E. Lewis.

Jean-Louis Chrétien, *The Call and the Response*. Translated with an introduction by Anne Davenport.

D. C. Schindler, *Han Urs von Balthasar and the Dramatic Structure of Truth: A Philosophical Investigation*.

Julian Wolfreys, ed., *Thinking Difference: Critics in Conversation*.

Allen Scult, *Being Jewish/Reading Heidegger: An Ontological Encounter*.

Richard Kearney, *Debates in Continental Philosophy: Conversations with Contemporary Thinkers*.

Jennifer Anna Gosetti-Ferencei, *Heidegger, Hölderlin, and the Subject of Poetic Language: Toward a New Poetics of Dasein*.

Jolita Pons, *Stealing a Gift: Kierkegaard's Pseudonyms and the Bible*.

Jean-Yves Lacoste, *Experience and the Absolute: Disputed Questions on the Humanity of Man*. Translated by Mark Raftery-Skehan.

Charles P. Bigger, *Between Chora and the Good: Metaphor's Metaphysical Neighborhood*.

Dominique Janicaud, *Phenomenology "Wide Open": After the French Debate*. Translated by Charles N. Cabral.

Ian Leask and Eoin Cassidy, eds., *Givenness and God: Questions of Jean-Luc Marion*.

Jacques Derrida, *Sovereignties in Question: The Poetics of Paul Celan*. Edited by Thomas Dutoit and Outi Pasanen.

William Desmond, *Is There a Sabbath for Thought? Between Religion and Philosophy*.

Bruce Ellis Benson and Norman Wirzba, eds., *The Phenomenology of Prayer*.

S. Clark Buckner and Matthew Statler, eds., *Styles of Piety: Practicing Philosophy after the Death of God*.

Kevin Hart and Barbara Wall, eds., *The Experience of God: A Postmodern Response*.

John Panteleimon Manoussakis, *After God: Richard Kearney and the Religious Turn in Continental Philosophy*.

John Martis, *Philippe Lacoue-Labarthe: Representation and the Loss of the Subject*.

Jean-Luc Nancy, *The Ground of the Image*.

Edith Wyschogrod, *Crossover Queries: Dwelling with Negatives, Embodying Philosophy's Others*.

Gerald Bruns, *On the Anarchy of Poetry and Philosophy: A Guide for the Unruly*.

Brian Treanor, *Aspects of Alterity: Levinas, Marcel, and the Contemporary Debate*.

Simon Morgan Wortham, *Counter-Institutions: Jacques Derrida and the Question of the University*.

Leonard Lawlor, *The Implications of Immanence: Toward a New Concept of Life*.

Clayton Crockett, *Interstices of the Sublime: Theology and Psychoanalytic Theory*.

Bettina Bergo, Joseph Cohen, and Raphael Zagury-Orly, eds., *Judeities: Questions for Jacques Derrida*. Translated by Bettina Bergo and Michael B. Smith.

Jean-Luc Marion, *On the Ego and on God: Further Cartesian Questions*. Translated by Christina M. Gschwandtner.

Jean-Luc Nancy, *Philosophical Chronicles*. Translated by Franson Manjali.

Jean-Luc Nancy, *Dis-Enclosure: The Deconstruction of Christianity*. Translated by Bettina Bergo, Gabriel Malenfant, and Michael B. Smith.

Andrea Hurst, *Derrida Vis-à-vis Lacan: Interweaving Deconstruction and Psychoanalysis*.

Jean-Luc Nancy, *Noli me tangere: On the Raising of the Body*. Translated by Sarah Clift, Pascale-Anne Brault, and Michael Naas.

Jacques Derrida, *The Animal That Therefore I Am*. Edited by Marie-Louise Mallet, translated by David Wills.

Jean-Luc Marion, *The Visible and the Revealed*. Translated by Christina M. Gschwandtner and others.

Michel Henry, *Material Phenomenology*. Translated by Scott Davidson.

Jean-Luc Nancy, *Corpus*. Translated by Richard A. Rand.

Joshua Kates, *Fielding Derrida*.

Michael Naas, *Derrida From Now On*.

Shannon Sullivan and Dennis J. Schmidt, eds., *Difficulties of Ethical Life*.